C000101932

Battleground 1

The Somme 1916

The Butte de Warlencourt
Martinpuich and Le Sars

Battleground series:

Frontispiece photo: Troops carrying 'elephant iron' through the shattered ruins of Le Sars.

Battleground Europe

The Somme 1916

The Butte de Warlencourt
Martinpuich and Le Sars

Bob Paterson

Series Editor
Nigel Cave

Pen & Sword
MILITARY

First published in Great Britain in 2022 by
Pen & Sword Military
An imprint of
Pen & Sword Books Ltd
Yorkshire – Philadelphia

Copyright © Bob Paterson 2022

ISBN 978 1 52676 446 1

The right of Bob Paterson to be identified as Author of this work
has been asserted by him in accordance with the Copyright,
Designs and Patents Act 1988.

A CIP catalogue record for this book is
available from the British Library.

All rights reserved. No part of this book may be reproduced or
transmitted in any form or by any means, electronic or mechanical
including photocopying, recording or by any information storage
and retrieval system, without permission from the Publisher
in writing.

Typeset by Mac Style
Printed and bound in the UK by CPI Group (UK) Ltd,
Croydon, CR0 4YY

Pen & Sword Books Limited incorporates the imprints of Atlas,
Archaeology, Aviation, Discovery, Family History, Fiction, History,
Maritime, Military, Military Classics, Politics, Select, Transport,
True Crime, Air World, Frontline Publishing, Leo Cooper,
Remember When, Seaforth Publishing, The Praetorian Press,
Wharncliffe Local History, Wharncliffe Transport, Wharncliffe
True Crime and White Owl.

For a complete list of Pen & Sword titles please contact

PEN & SWORD BOOKS LIMITED
47 Church Street, Barnsley, South Yorkshire, S70 2AS, England
E-mail: enquiries@pen-and-sword.co.uk
Website: www.pen-and-sword.co.uk

Or

PEN AND SWORD BOOKS
1950 Lawrence Rd, Havertown, PA 19083, USA
E-mail: Uspen-and-sword@casematepublishers.com
Website: www.penandswordbooks.com

Contents

List of Maps

Series Editor's Introduction

The Butte de Warlencourt today appears to be a lone, mysterious hillock in the Somme landscape, seemingly out of place amidst the undulating countryside. And indeed it is, in that it is a human creation, for what purpose is unclear – possibly a Romano-Gallic burial mound – and dates back hundreds of years, made at a time when it was all but surrounded by forest, although on its north side it was close by a significant Roman road.

Over the centuries following its creation it would certainly have witnessed the passage of great armies, most recently during the Franco-Prussian War and, memorably, in the First World War, when its symbolic significance has turned out to outweigh its wartime military value.

By the official end of the Battle of the Somme 1916, the promise of the offensive was engulfed in the mud and destruction of the battlefield and had cost the maiming or loss of hundreds of thousands of lives. Amidst the carnage the Butte stood out almost as a shining beacon and conveniently marked the limit of the British advance along the Bapaume road. Stripped of its vegetation, the chalk that forms a notable part of its bulk served to highlight its dominating presence over this part of the Somme. This description is not some form of literary hyperbole, as references to its threatening appearance are to be found in several memoirs, amongst which is Norman Gladden's (who served in the Northumberland Fusiliers) outstanding *The Somme 1916*. A mile or two further south, in similar conditions to that around the Butte, Sidney Rogerson spent time in November before Le Transloy and wrote in his great classic, *Twelve Days: The Somme November 1916*, of his experiences as a company commander in the 2nd West Yorks in the line there. I would strongly urge readers of this book to follow it up by turning to these two memoirs; currently, Gladden's is not in print but Rogerson's is. From these you will get a vivid description and consequently a better understanding of the experience of infantry soldiers in the late autumn of 1916 in these Somme fields.

It appears to be an unfortunate fact that the coverage of the last two months or so of the Battle of the Somme 1916 is not, generally, extensive: histories and accounts tend to concentrate on the preparations for and the opening day or two of the battle. There are exceptions, of course; High Wood and Delville Wood, particularly when they both came into popular consciousness on 14 July, at the opening of the second phase of the British part of the offensive, often get considerable attention. And plenty has been written about 15 September, the opening of the third phase, above all notable for the first use of tanks on a battlefield. But when all is considered the last two months seem almost to have disappeared without trace into the mud and slime that characterised these last eight or so weeks of intensive fighting.

Popular interest in the battle in recent decades, perhaps dating from Martin Middlebrook's outstanding 1971 book, *The First Day of the Somme* (and which I think has never been out of print since), which was followed in the eighties by a series of books on the Pals battalions, has tended to concentrate on the British line on 1 July 1916 and the tragic events surrounding that date. This trend has been supported by the continual development of facilities at significant memorials (eg the Thiepval Memorial, the Ulster Tower) and remains of the battlefield on that line (eg the Newfoundland Memorial Park and the Lochnagar Crater), all of which provide a handy basis for many of the numerous school parties (in particular), most of which have a very limited period of time to 'see' the Somme battlefield. I should be careful of pushing this too far, but this is the strong impression that I get.

It was not always so. It is notable that in the early post war years that the Butte evoked considerable interest; for example, it was a prominent stop in what was termed 'the King's pilgrimage' to the battlefields in 1922. It inspired several of the war artists. Situated as it is by the main road between Bapaume and Albert, the main east west route through the British sector, countless thousands of members of the British Expeditionary Force could not have failed to take note of it. Even during the war and immediately afterwards, when the French government was considering which places should be preserved as memorials of the conflict, the Butte de Warlencourt was one of only a handful of locations along the whole of the front in France that were considered suitable for retention. In one report or other, in the British sector of the Somme, these were identified as the 'twin' craters at La Boisselle (Lochnagar and Y Sap), Thiepval Chateau and the Butte de Warlencourt.

Indeed, when I first came to the Somme in August 1968 with my father for a very brief visit, we were unarmed with any guide – at that time the only one, I think, was the out of print, post war, Michelin guide. Rose Coombs' invaluable *Before Endeavours Fade* was not available then, first appearing in 1976. Approaching Albert, our base, from Bapaume, we stopped at Warlencourt British Cemetery, my first Somme cemetery; whilst there my father pointed out the tree and shrub covered Butte, off in the middle distance to the south west, and explained its significance and talked of the famous 'Durham Crosses' that had been erected on or close to its summit. It was the first battlefield remnant of the Somme that I saw, although we did not visit on that occasion, given its jungle-like appearance, the fact that it was private property and the need for refreshments after a long but interesting journey from Ypres. When we did eventually manage to do so, about ten years later, it was a struggle to get through the vegetation (having negotiated the broken-down barbed wire fence) to reach the summit and when we got there it was difficult to appreciate its dominance of the immediate area and any of its distant views. Of the original crosses there were no signs, although there remained a rather sad looking wooden cross erected by a German unit, I think in 1944.

Probably since the outbreak of the Second World War it is fair to say that the Butte has been very much a 'minority' interest for most battlefield visitors. Its immediate future was secured by the Western Front Association in 1990, and its security and developments to make it more instructive, accessible and generally visitor friendly have been further greatly enhanced since it was sold in 2018: it well deserves to be, once again, as it was in the pre Second World War years, one of the essential stops for those touring the Somme battlefields of 1916.

This is to be much welcomed, as, of course, is this book, the first new entry into the Battleground Europe series of books on the Somme 1916 for about fifteen years (with the exception of those on the French army by the late Dave O'Mara). One can hope that it will help to encourage visitors to the Somme to this iconic spot, a symbol of the endurance and courage of the soldiers of the Somme in that rain-sodden autumn of 1916, a silent witness to grim determination, fortitude and resilience; yet also of dashed hopes, unrealistic expectations and much human misery. From the top of the Butte, now cleared of obstructing vegetation, it is possible to view the ground over which men from Britain and South Africa struggled against the resolute German defenders. The narrative in the book provides an account of the events that took place in these French fields from mid September to the official end of the battle, in mid November. The tour section puts you 'on the ground', providing the topographical context that makes understanding what was going on and why features had a particular value that much easier.

Those who fought here in the late autumn of 1916 have, for whatever reason, often been neglected by posterity, their actions summarised in a line or two referring to the generally very poor conditions and of an offensive that had completely stalled in the mud. They deserve more respect than that and it is to be hoped that Bob Paterson's book will play its part in making their stories and actions better known and appreciated.

Nigel Cave
Ratcliffe College, March 2022.

Introduction

My father was ninety when he died. Born in 1908, he could remember as a youngster the effects that the Battles of Loos and the Somme had on the people of his beloved Dundee. He told me some war bits and pieces when I was growing up but, as for most adolescents, there were far more important things in life to worry about rather than his, dare I say, what were at the time rather boring stories. Watching Dundee FC and playing golf at the plethora of championship courses close to Dundee were in my opinion far more exciting. Which was better: a story about something in India that seemed light years before or a once in a lifetime birdie on the last hole on the Championship course at St Andrews watched by the multitude of tourists who swarm to the home of golf? One story however that did stick from my very early years was that he and his mother were once amongst others summoned to a school gym hall where a list of recent war dead was read out alphabetically; every attendee panicked until the announcer went past your surname's initial in the alphabet. Whether this was true or not I have no idea. I see no reason for it not to be and why he would make it up; maybe this was one of the local methods of getting out information. His father, my grandfather, who was also called Bob, did not serve in the Great War as he worked in a protected trade, i.e. shipbuilding. He had worked as a riveter in the Harland and Wolff shipyard in Belfast where, according to family folk lore, amongst the various ships he worked on was the fated RMS *Titanic*.

My father, Bob senior, served in the Second World War in the RAF. He was called up whilst on holiday in the exotic town of Blairgowrie in Perthshire in July 1940, Blairgowrie a distant eighteen miles from his home. He was posted to RAF Manston in Kent in September 1940, just in time for the beginning of the end of the

My father – Robert (Bob) Senior. (*Author*)

R.A.F. Form 2520/25

RELEASE AUTHORISATION

PART I
To be completed in Unit except when marked**.

Rank   LAC   Number 1058625

Initials   R.   Surname PATERSON

Release of the above-named airman is
hereby authorised as a Class A release,
and he is relegated to Class G1 of the
Reserve.
The effective date of release (i.e. last day of
service) is   15.1.46

It is hereby certified that the above airman served in the
R.A.F. on whole-time service during the following periods :

From   To

15.8.1940   17.10.45

(Date of departure from
Dispersal Centre)

He is granted   90   days' leave on release commencing the
day following the date of departure from the Dispersal Centre.

R.A.F. Form 2520/25
(continued)

RELEASE AUTHORISATION
(continued)

PART II
Instructions to Class B releases to report for Employment
You have been released to take up employment

as a
(M. of L. code number   )

Delete   and are to report within seven days from your
one   departure from this Dispersal Centre to the
of   following Employment Exchange
these   OR
            with Messrs.

            of
            whom you are to report within seven days from
            your departure from this Dispersal Centre.

You will ordinarily be required to commence work on the
expiration of your leave, but you may if you desire commence
at any earlier time.

PART III

NO. 104 P.D.C.
17 OCT 1945
WEDNESFORD

E.S.B.

for A.O. i/c Records

Dispersal Centre Stamp.

My father's RAF release papers at the end of his war service. (*Author*)

Battle of Britain. Leading Aircraftman
Paterson was officially released from
full service on 15 January 1946; from
late 1942 onwards he had served in
far more distant places, such as East
Africa, Bombay, Ceylon and more. In
later years he loved travelling with my
mother, making Southern Rhodesia
their home before returning to Scotland
in 1956. As for so many who have
developed a deep interest in the Great
War in middle age, he was no longer
there any longer to answer the queries
or questions I had when my interest
had been kindled. His undocumented
stories of life in Dundee during that war
and of the town's beloved Black Watch
had simply passed with him, as had
numerous Second World War tales from
the UK and the Far East.

A moderate interest in the war was
promoted into a full-time passion,
seemingly from out of the blue. When

Private Hugh Carmichael, 4th
Battalion Cameron Highlanders:
killed in action on 17 May 1915.
(*Author*).

xii

undertaking the sad task of clearing the home of my wife's father, we stumbled upon paperwork in a black bin bag that had been destined for the skip. Investigation of it revealed details of a great uncle, Hugh Carmichael, who was killed at Festubert in May 1915: an uncle we never knew existed. Determined to be the first relations to visit his final resting place, a visit to le Touret Cemetery (near Neuve-Chapelle) did not lead to a grave but a name on the wall (Panels 41/42), one of the missing. It turns out that Hugh had been found, identified and buried in Festubert in May 1915; but, sadly, his grave itself became another casualty of the war, almost certainly during the 1918 Battle of the Lys.

This visit to France provided the opportunity to visit the Somme battlefields, all located within easy driving distances from the small town of Albert, more or less at the centre rear of the British line. This was the start of a love affair with the hallowed Somme ground, mud and all: soon after a small house was purchased in Morval – towards the south-eastern limit of the British advance in 1916 – and resulted in

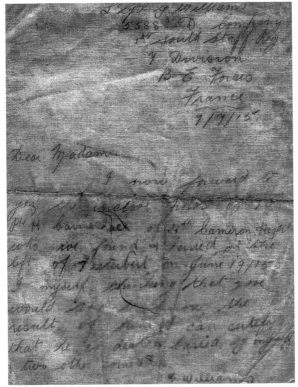

A letter from Lance Corporal G Williams, dated 7 July 1915, stating that he had buried Hugh Carmichael 'left of Festubert' on 19 June 1915. (*Author*)

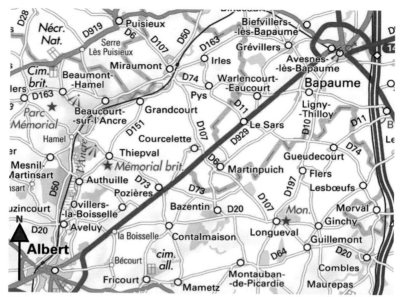

The area of the Somme battlefields from July to November 1916. (Approximate scale 1 cm = 1000 m)

a seriously big, unplanned and far from budgeted restoration project. Morval, with a small population of ninety and, like so many of these small Somme villages, with now fifty percent or more fewer people than there were in 1914, is located eighteen kilometres almost due east from Albert. It was captured by the allies on 25 September 1916 as part of the aptly named Battle of Morval.

The Battle of the Somme 1916 in the area covered by this book effectively commenced on 1 July 1916 at the Lochnagar Crater, close to the main D929 Albert to Bapaume road. The fighting on and fallout of the first of July has since been covered from almost every conceivable angle. About seventy-five days later and approximately eight kilometres up this road, the small village of Martinpuich was taken. A further sixty-five days later the battle officially came to an end (at least so far as the British were concerned – the Germans and the French both have different end dates) with the front line being situated at an infamous mound, the Butte de Warlencourt, a further four kilometres or so from Martinpuich and just past Le Sars. From 1 July the advance down the road had taken the men of the BEF forward some twelve kilometres over 140 days – progress at roughly 600 metres a week. It was, of course, far from the planned and very much hoped for sweeping breakthrough.

Lochnagar Crater, conveniently quite close to the main road, became a popular place to visit; threatened with being filled in, it was saved by Mr Richard Dunning in 1978. It provides a magnet to visitors and gives a clear indication of the sheer power of the weaponry – in this case a mine – of the war, as well as being a poignant reminder of the events of 1 July. The same 'popularity' cannot be said to apply to the infamous hillock held by the Germans where the fighting finished in November, the undefeated Butte de Warlencourt. It is pretty much unknown and certainly much, much less visited. Is it just too far up the D929, the road which was to be made so famous by Sir Harry Lauder's 1917 song 'Keep right on to the end of the road'? The crater has the power to awe, because it is so unusual and is such an indication of the power that mankind could apply in war and which would leave such a permanent scar; the Butte, even if manmade, was not the consequence of a great blast and, what is more, had been part of the landscape for centuries: no, it does not have the same visual impact. The Butte is the vertical opposite of the crater; the latter is sixty feet below ground level and the former sixty feet above and can be seen from miles around. And yet …. Within a few days of 1 July the fighting had moved on from around Lochnagar Crater whilst that around the Butte, including evocative 'signpost' names such as The Pimple, Snag Trench and The Tail, went on for several weeks and was as fierce as at any time during the battle. The conditions, however, in that Somme autumn were simply horrendous, with some veterans

The infamous Butte de Warlencourt after the war had moved on, its crest dominated by memorial crosses.

saying that they were worse than at Passchendaele the following year. As Lochnagar Crater symbolises to many the opening of the Battle of the Somme, the slight, ominous, battered ruin of the Butte, surrounded by its sea of mud, a beacon of the determination of both sides, symbolises the tenacity, doggedness and enduring spirit of the men of the Somme (despite all) at the end of that battle at the fag end of 1916.

The aim in this book to cover the fighting in the period from mid-September 1916 to the end of the battle of the Somme on 18 November 1916 from the area on the right hand (south) side of the D929 heading northwards from Martinpuich to the Butte, just past the village of Le Sars. This advance, covering the capture of Martinpuich, Eaucourt l'Abbaye (modern day l'Abbaye d'Eaucourt) and Le Sars, stopped in the

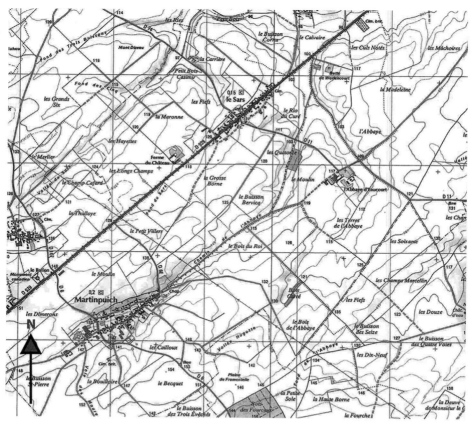

Area of fighting from Martinpuich to the Butte de Warlencourt. (Approximate scale 1 cm = 200 m)

shadows of the Butte and saw the British facing two enemies, a stubborn determined German force, and the horrendous ground conditions – the French, over to the right, faced their similar iconic location before the mass of St Pierre Vaast Wood. The weather on the Somme that autumn of 1916 was far from good and the rain, with its inevitable impact on the ground conditions, was incessant; however, the desire of both sides to hold a tenable line and a suitable starting point for future operations at the end of the battle meant that the fighting had to go on regardless of the atrocious weather and the effect it was having on the troops.

The early success of the opening stages of the Battle of Flers-Courcelette in mid-September saw the capture of the villages of Flers and Martinpuich, both taken in a day. Less than two weeks later nearby Morval fell in a matter of hours. These successes contrast greatly with what was to happen in the remaining weeks of the battle, a seemingly never ending, lethal slog. The Butte de Warlencourt, standing out from the surrounding landscape, not least because of the extensive chalk in its bulk and giving it a characteristic glimmer of white, came to symbolise to many of the troops the fighting in this sector and it remained unconquered, however tantalisingly close the men of the BEF got to capturing it. To those involved in the struggle here it almost became an end in itself, the bigger issues of the battle too remote to be of great interest. This book investigates the fighting from Martinpuich to the Butte, admittedly in a concise format – based largely on the operational activity of the divisions involved, accompanied by tours on the ground, which I hope will help the visitor to appreciate and understand to some degree what those soldiers of autumn 1916 sought to achieve and what they endured.

Many an unsuspecting driver will have driven this section of the Post Road (as it was often known during the war) from the turn off to Martinpuich to the Butte de Warlencourt hundreds of times without realising what happened here in the autumn of 1916. The appearance of these peaceful, relatively routine and mundane fields seen today are far, far removed from those same fields, the scene of such heroism and such misery, in the autumn of 1916.

Bob Paterson
Dundee, Autumn 2021

Acknowledgements

Like any book about the 1916 Battle of the Somme, the people who the author must acknowledge the most are now long departed. I of course refer to the troops of all ranks, race and religion who took part in this iconic, historic event over a century ago; and to those who left the records, oral, visual and written, for those of us who come afterwards.

As stated by Nigel Cave in his excellent book in the same series about Beaumont Hamel, this book is mainly researched from others who wrote accounts of the war and those who wrote divisional histories. Sources – for example battalion and regimental histories, memoirs and relevant documents – have been studied, the results of which I have endeavoured to present in a manner that I hope you find enjoyable, useful, and informative. Behind many of the battle accounts and stories are my personal thoughts, having spent many years on the Somme based in my house at Morval. For a student of the battle such a base is invaluable: the Somme battlefields of 1916 are relatively compact and today's major sights can be easily visited by car in a day (albeit something of a whistle stop tour). To be accurate, villages or hamlets such as Martinpuich, Le Sars, Eaucourt l'Abbaye and, indeed, Morval, are not located in the *département* of the Somme but in its neighbour, the *département* of the Pas de Calais (and even this division is subject to periodic administrative tinkering). But the Somme will do for this book.

We should always remember the sacrifices of the men and women of the period of the Great War, so many of whose lives were dramatically and permanently changed by it, directly or indirectly. The enduring work of the Imperial/Commonwealth War Graves Commission (CWGC) in keeping their cemeteries and grave sites and memorials in the area in perfect condition here as elsewhere can be nothing else but stirring and very impressive. Its website is a very valuable resource tool for any student of the Great War. Elsewhere on the internet, which seems to have taken over so much of our lives, there are numerous sites that provide a wealth of relevant information; but one must tread carefully and ensure that the information placed there by well-meaning people is indeed accurate.

My sincere appreciation goes to the mayors of Warlencourt-Eaucourt, Martinpuich and Morval for their assistance, particularly keeping one on the right side of the intricacies of French protocol, which at times can be lengthy and certainly different to ours in the UK. I have known Lucien Guise, a former Mayor of Warlencourt, now retired from that post, for several years. He has been most helpful and welcoming; although appreciating that the Butte de Warlencourt is in his commune, he and others in the area fully recognise that the French never fought here in 1916. The French army's sterling efforts at the time were applied some distance south of the Butte. Monsieur Guise sees the site as a British focal point, though of course warmly welcoming visitors from all countries to his commune and is delighted to see the Butte being loved and well looked after.

Charles and Blanche Crossan of Warlencourt have been of immense help. My wife Julia and I first met them in the *Mairie* in Warlencourt in my Western Front Association (WFA) days and they have now become the closest of friends. They know everything about everything, especially the history of the area, and are more than happy to pass on their knowledge of Warlencourt and Bapaume and its surrounds.

A great friend over the last sixty years, Derek Muir, smiled nicely at me when I asked for a favour; so he got the job of drawing the base maps for the walks and vehicle tours. We wanted these maps to be clean and not too cluttered. Derek has successfully done this by hand, relying on pens that were put away some forty years ago in his academic days. A keen walker and a Munro climbing guru in Scotland, Derek accompanied me when drafting the walks and the vehicle tour and was the major help in pulling the details of our escapades together. The GPS details given (and much more) are all his fine work; as are the bulk of the common-sense comments in the actual walks. The only thing I do not like about Derek is he never lets me beat him at golf.

Following on from the maps for the walks: for other maps, pictures and related material, I should acknowledge the indispensable contribution of Microsoft and its various programs. To the serious user these products

Derek Muir (on the left!) looking well. No prizes for guessing the location. (*Author*)

justify their monthly subscription fees. On the internet eBay has proved its value. Perhaps already past its halcyon days, it has proved ideal for obtaining Great War memorabilia, such as images, trench maps and related material. I have never been slow to ask the Somme (and more) photography genius Stevie Kerr for pictures of the area; his pictures of the Somme are wonderful, especially those taken from the air, and several of his efforts are contained in the book. For further details of Stephen's work, have a look at his website www.skphotoscom.co.uk

The immense knowledge of library staff at the University of Dundee has been most helpful in my research. I had the pleasure of studying a few years ago for the MA in British First World War studies at the University of Birmingham. This was no doubt one of the most enjoyable periods of my life and it certainly enhanced my knowledge of the First World War. It was a true pleasure speaking to and learning from the likes of Professors Gary Sheffield and Peter Simpkins. One stalwart at the course was the one and only Rob Thomson, who has since became a great friend. Rob's thoughts and straight to the point advice have been most helpful in the preparation of this book.

'Mad dog' Henry eyes up his next victim. (*Author*)

Over my working career I have always been a figures man. I of course refer to numbers before being accused of anything else. The role of proof reading and grammar checking in this book is, naturally, a major concern and always best done by 'new' eyes. Paul Donaldson has been the proof reading and grammar star; however, any errors, grammatical or otherwise, rest entirely with the author. Paul visited the Somme for the first time recently and it was great to have his thoughts on the contents as a 'Somme novice' and consequently to include one or two items of information that he would have found useful as a first-time visitor.

Another star is of course my wife Julia. She has played a major role in getting to where we are. Without doubt she is the best person on whom to bounce ideas and has been vital in reading first drafts and looking at the contents and words in different ways. She quickly brings anyone back down to earth – a very useful attribute indeed. Thank you also to my daughter Suzanne, a qualified museum curator. At times she has far too much of her father in her, with lots of traits, good and (and very occasionally) bad. She was also a big help in cutting down words and getting to the point. Never to be left out, son Christy has a great ability in dissecting contents into keep, reject and rewrite. He reads the book as a reader, ie what does the reader want and expect to see. The family involvement has, therefore, been high, a true team effort, each bringing their own attribute to the table. I suppose I am now bound to mention as part of the family mad dog Henry, the Skye terrier who accompanies us everywhere, not least on the battlefields. Once met, he can never be forgotten: In the house a perfect canine gentleman, whilst outside he will fight his own shadow. Over a century ago he could have taken the Butte on his own. If you see him wandering battlefields, please say hello.

Finally, my thanks to all at Pen and Sword in Barnsley, to the series editor Nigel Cave for all his input, edits, and encouragement. Nigel has a wealth of knowledge and experience and passes this on readily. Being my first ever attempt to write a book, he was a vital assistance in matters of the series' protocols, rules and regulations, both written and unwritten.

There will be people I have omitted, and I am truly sorry if I have done so; hopefully they know of my appreciation. There must be one, final thank you, however, and the best always come last: to Private Hugh Carmichael, killed at Festubert on 17 May 1915. This was a guy we never knew existed and, without finding his name in those old, discarded papers in a bin bag, destined for destruction, I really doubt if we would have made that first visit to the Somme. Thanks, Hugh, for everything.

Chapter One

The Somme Battle 1916:
September to the Battle's End

An overview

The 1916 Battle of the Somme was the bloodiest battle of the Great War. Between the end of June 1916 and the final stages of the battle in November 1916, the British lost a total of around 420,000 men, the French 204,000, and the Germans about 465,000, possibly more. The first day of the battle on 1 July had seen more than 57,000 British casualties alone and had resulted in no significant success except on the southern side of the BEF's front, alongside the French, the latter of whom had what could be described as a good day, especially south of the river. The long hoped-for cavalry breakthrough in July did not happen and, apart from success on a larger scale in mid-July, progress thereafter was gradual as the summer of 1916 turned to autumn.

In the vicinity of Martinpuich (and thus the Butte de Warlencourt), the early days in September saw Guillemont (finally – it had taken over seven weeks) and Ginchy fall into allied hands, with some ground taken in High Wood. Sir Douglas Haig in his Despatches stated that his limited success of early September exceeded anything that had been achieved since the promise of 14 July. The stage was now set for the third major stage of the battle, where Fourth Army was to attack the German defences between Morval, on the right of the front adjoining the French army, to east of Pozières, straddling the main Albert to Bapaume Road – known then as the Post Road, dating from when this old Roman road was used for a horse-ridden courier service. The Battle of Flers-Courcelette started on 15 September and was the biggest operation undertaken by the British since the opening day of the battle some two and a half months earlier – and they did not do it alone, for the French army had begun extending its front south of the river, starting with a significant attack on 3 September.

The opening of the offensive on 15 September was a significant date for another reason: it witnessed the introduction of a new weapon of war, what some called 'woodlice', one of the many nicknames for the mechanically unreliable armoured vehicle that soon became generally known as tanks. Having prepared the line with the capture

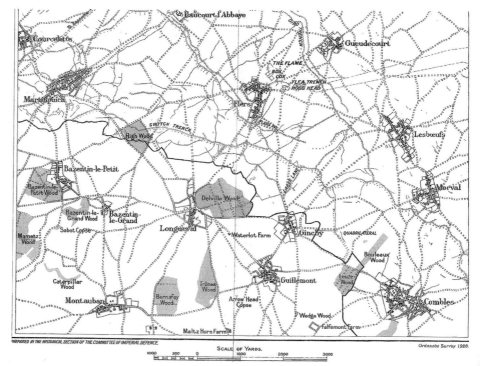

Area of Fourth Army operations: 15 September 1916. (*Author*)

of Guillemont and Ginchy (and, finally, Delville Wood) Haig hoped for a breakthrough and a return to open warfare and was prepared to use any weapon at his disposal, including the arguably premature use of the new, armoured 'caterpillar'; he even toyed with the idea of firing the Messines mines (which, memorably, were fired on 7 June 1917) as a diversionary strategy. Initial results saw, amongst others, the targets of Martinpuich and High Wood captured after some two years of German occupation, but several other objectives were not. The results were disappointing, and the role and effect of the tank perceived as mixed but holding promise for the future – Haig ordered a thousand of them.

The final phase of the Battle of the Somme began a fortnight later, at the end of September 1916, this ultimately breaking down into countless minor battles and an obligatory desire to straighten the line, with the notable exception of a final push on the Ancre Heights. On the left of Fourth Army, Eaucourt l'Abbaye, Le Sars and the Butte de Warlencourt became the main objectives: but the British now faced two enemies, the Germans and the mud. The autumn weather brought a change for the worse as persistent rain transformed the battlefield into what Ernst Junger described as 'a landscape of primeval mud'.

By mid-November 1916, when the battle officially ended, the nearby town of Bapaume, an optimistic first day objective for the cavalry, remained securely in German hands. Eaucourt l'Abbaye had been taken, as had Le Sars; however, the gleaming dome of the Butte de Warlencourt, resplendent with the chalk that largely comprised it after the surface soil had been blasted away, stood proud and undefeated after several ferocious British attempts to capture it, becoming almost an icon of these final, sodden weeks of the offensive. Rain, cold, slow reliefs and lack of almost any food, all endured in the most ghastly ground conditions, had made these episodes and more a severe test of endurance. So bad were things that it was not unusual for a stretcher to require eight bearers, whilst runners, carrying no heavy equipment, were taking up to six hours to cover a thousand yards, about 150 metres an hour. On a normal day the reader could perhaps walk four miles in an hour at a fairly brisk rate, three miles at a leisurely stroll. As the battle struggled on the front was rarely at any one moment clearly defined, often comprising tenuously linked shell holes (and the Germans and the French faced a

The Somme battlefields in October 1916. (*Digital History Archive*)

similar situation), leading to inevitable confusion. At times officers led and men followed but both were in a fog of uncertainty.

The History of the 50th Division was written by Everard Wyrall (1878–1933, himself a soldier who had served in the South African War, the Great War and was involved in the post war conflict in Afghanistan in 1919). He wrote some twenty divisional and regimental histories, several of which were multi volume affairs. So he had experience of the military – and, more importantly, the war – as well as being a military historian of repute. Thus he knew of what he wrote. The 50th (Northumbrian) Division was heavily involved in this area and at this time; his description below has the evident attributes of the soldier's eye.

'… the first winter on the Somme was fast approaching. The battlefield, under torrents of rain, had already assumed that forlorn and desolate appearance which ever after remained, burnt in upon one's brain – a vision of living torture. Every village wrested from the enemy since the 1st of July was now but a mass of tumbled or tottering masonry, each day and night witnessing further ruination; every road had been wrecked by mines or was pock-marked by shell-holes; every wood had been so torn, disfigured and disintegrated that "wood" was but a misnomer. The ingenuity of Man had rendered Nature abortive, for the very face of the earth was changed, and was ever changing, becoming more brutal, more savage than in its primeval state. Farms, quarries, windmills had gone the way of the villages and the woods wrecked and ruined by the awful holocaust of high explosive and shrapnel. The very earth stank of gas and was discoloured by the fumes from the bursting of gas shells. The countryside (if so it could be named) was a vast mass of shell-holes overlapping each other in the tens of thousands; already they were full of noisome water, putrid from the dead bodies of friend or foe to whom no burial had been given. The foetid stench from the rotting carcases of horses, or the poor remains of Briton or German torn from their hastily-dug graves by shell fire and tossed here and there to await the mercy of fresh interment, filled the nostrils as one passed to or from the front line.

But as yet (though conditions were bad enough) the full horrors of that first winter on the Somme had not been experienced; towards the end of October the mud in many front line and communication trenches was only some two feet in depth ; duck-board tracks (in those Divisional areas where the staff had been lucky enough to obtain the materials to build them) had not yet

Sleighs used for transporting the wounded through the mud at Le Sars, October 1916. (*Fonds des albums Valois* – Pas de Calais)

begun to sink out of sight; men and horses and mules had not yet been drowned in mud and shell-holes as some were later; and troops coming out of the line still had the appearance of soldiers, not erstwhile Robinson Crusoes who, burrowing in the earth, had become sodden through and covered in mud from tip to toe.'

When people visit the Somme they usually drive along this stretch of the Post Road as they hasten to the 'popular' visitor magnets, usually related to 1 July, with only the haziest of ideas of the slough of despond that was the scene of the dying last couple of months of the great Somme offensive of 1916.

Chapter Two

Mid-September success – Martinpuich is taken

The background

Before the subject area of this book can be tackled it is necessary, albeit very briefly, to put the situation in the context of what was happening on the wider Somme battlefield.

At the end of August 1916 von Falkenhayn was sacked as Chief of the German General Staff, the final straw in his downfall being the declaration of war on Germany by Romania (disastrously, as it turned out, for the latter); he was replaced by what became known as the 'duumvirate' (i.e. command team) of Hindenburg and Ludendorff. In early September the French extended their front south of the Somme by a further ten kilometres. Finally, after weeks of severe, bloody but fairly localised fighting dating back to the immediate aftermath of the offensive of 14 July, Delville Wood, Guillemont and then Ginchy fell to the British. The capture of these bastions of German resistance were necessary preconditions to providing a satisfactory start line for a general offensive in this area. Thiepval, the key village on the heights south of the Ancre river, the tactical key to the German position on the Somme, remained in German hands; but parts of the dominating ridge that ran more or less south east to High Wood and beyond and that bears its name had, bit by bit, agonising step by agonising step, been captured. Indeed this 'nibbling' had already had an impact. At a conference of very senior German officers on the Western Front at Cambrai on 8 September with the new German High Command, the idea was discussed that new, shortened and well prepared lines to the rear should be commenced, which were to become known collectively, by the British at least, as the Hindenburg Line.

The British contribution to the third stage of the Somme Offensive, in particular of Rawlinson's Fourth Army, was to capture the German line between Morval and Le Sars, a distance as the crow flies of some eight kilometres. On the left General Gough's Reserve Army would cover the shoulder of the attack, at the same time continuing to press against Thiepval. Thus the Canadian Corps took the offensive north – and just south – of the Bapaume road, encompassing Courcelette, with its 2nd and 3rd (Canadian) Divisions in the line. Rawlinson deployed three corps for his Army's part in the attack: to the south of the Bapaume road and on the left of the Army front, was Lieutenant General Sir William Pulteney's III Corps, having in the line, from right to left, the 47th (1/2nd London), the 50th (Northumbrian) – two theoretically territorial divisions – and the 15th (Scottish) Divisions, a New Army Formation from 'K2'. This chapter is concerned with this Corps and of these three divisions, in particular the action that was to see the successful capture

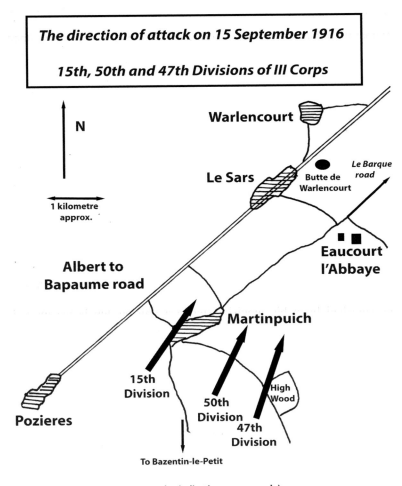

The attack of 15 September 1916: the 15th, 50th and 47th Divisions.

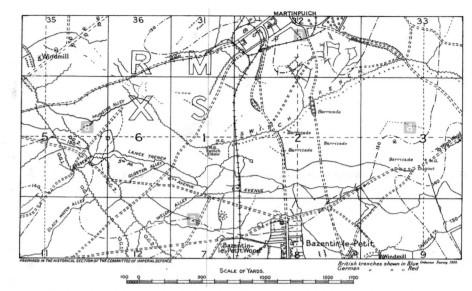

The location of trenches in the Martinpuich area, dated 30th July 1916. (*Author*)

of Martinpuich and its surrounds by the 15th Division, ably assisted by the 50th Division.

Like the 47th (1/2nd London) Division, their III Corps colleagues, the 15th (Scottish) Division, arrived on the Somme some time before the battle. After a march of over sixty miles, the division took over the left sector of III Corps' front from the 23rd Division on 8 August 1916. Their sector was in two sections, the right section, from the Bazentin-le Petit to Martinpuich road to Gloster Alley, under 46 Brigade; and the left section, from Gloster Alley to Munster Alley, under 45 Brigade. In reserve was 44 Brigade.

The Division had hardly settled in the area when orders were issued for an attack on the German trenches south of Martinpuich on 12 August. The 15th (Scottish) Division had to capture that part of the German front known as the Switch Line from the Bazentin-Martinpuich road to Munster Alley. The assault would take place at night and, to assist in the task, tapes were laid down in No Man's Land. For four days prior to the assault the enemy's trenches were subjected to a massive bombardment; when the position was ultimately captured it was found that this bombardment had destroyed many of the German trenches.

At 10.30 pm on 12 August the assault was delivered. Ultimately, although the 15th Division did not gain all its objectives, there were important gains, so that from the captured ground an extensive view was

Captain William Bryce Binnie

Captain Binnie moved up the ranks as the war progressed, finishing it as an acting lieutenant colonel, in the course of which he was awarded the MC and bar and survived the war, dying in 1963. Binnie was a highly successful architect and after the war was amongst those who worked with the then Imperial War Graves Commission. The Nieuport Memorial, which commemorates 552 British officers and men who were killed in Allied operations on the Belgian coast during the First World War and have no known grave, was designed by him. Twenty of those commemorated served with the Royal Naval Division and were killed or mortally wounded during the siege of Antwerp in October 1914. Almost all the remainder fell in heavy fighting in the region of Nieuport in the summer of 1917. The memorial is constructed of Euville limestone and stands eight metres high. The lions at each point of the triangular platform were designed by Charles Sergeant Jagger, a celebrated British sculptor and decorated veteran of the Western Front. The memorial was officially unveiled in July 1928.

The Nieuport Memorial to the Missing. (*Marc Ryckaert*)

He and his colleague Claude Ferrier went on to design the eye wateringly expensive east stand of Arsenal Football Club's former stadium at Highbury. The stand, containing the famous Marble Halls, is now a Grade II listed building. Built in 1936 to compliment

9

The East Stand at Highbury. (*Wikimedia Commons*)

the Victorian houses in the surrounding area, it was constructed in the Art Deco style, very popular between the wars, by Binnie and Ferrier. The stand was officially opened on 24 October 1936, when Arsenal hosted Grimsby Town.

obtained from where observers were able to direct fire on enemy troops around the area of Martinpuich. It is also worth highlighting a local action that took place five days later. Improvisation, as is so often the case in small unit actions, helped to save the day, in this case involving a captain in the Black Watch who, in due course, was to have a connection with Arsenal Football Club.

On 17 August an attack was made by three companies of the 7th Queen's Own Cameron Highlanders (7/Camerons) of 44 Brigade. Leaving their trench at 8.55 am accompanied by the usual barrage, they easily entered the enemy's trenches. Several Germans surrendered at once, and the work of consolidation was promptly begun. An hour later the Germans started a bombing attack against Switch [sometimes named Witch's] Elbow on the right. This was at first successful, and the enemy retook the Elbow. Their further advance was stopped after a vigorous counterattack and by the forming of a block in the trench just east of the Elbow. The 7/Camerons had run out of bombs when this German attack commenced and they endeavoured to defend the captured trench with the only weapons in their possession, their picks and shovels even, as you do in extreme circumstances, throwing them at the advancing Germans! The Camerons held on to their gains and at 2.00 pm a company of the 8th Seaforth Highlanders (8/Seaforths) of 44 Brigade arrived. With the assistance of the Seaforths a further attack was organised on the Switch Elbow. By this time all of the officers of the Camerons present had become casualties. Captain Binnie, with two companies of the 9th Black Watch (Royal Highlanders) (9/BW), was sent forward and immediately began preparations to recapture The Elbow; it was retaken with very little trouble, Captain Binnie thereby earning mentions in several histories for his efforts.

Martinpuich captured by the 15th (Scottish) Division

By the end of August the British line had been pushed forward to the rising ground south of Martinpuich, from where the ground sloped gently downwards to the village, its objective in the main attack of 15 September. From this elevated position the village was to be subjected to a tremendous bombardment. However, with nearby High Wood still in German possession, the new British front came under very accurate fire.

Four jumping-off trenches were dug in front of the line for the main attack, bearing respectively the British staple diet names of Egg, Bacon, Ham and Liver; candidate names these days might well be Pepperoni, Muesli, Vegan and Latte trenches! The most detailed preparations and instructions were issued for the attack on 15 September. On 7 September, 45 and 46 Brigades were withdrawn to rest and train for the attack, whilst 44 and 103 Brigades (the latter attached from the 34th Division) took their place in the line. 45 and 46 Brigades spent eight days rehearsing the assault in the rear over ground marked out to represent the enemy trenches to be attacked; preparation was meticulous.

The 15th (Scottish) Division were to approach Martinpuich from the south west, assisted by a new mechanical invention; the tanks had arrived on the battlefield, to dominate conventional warfare for the rest of the twentieth century. The Division had to capture two lines of trenches and then establish a line on the south western side of the village. The attack would be carried out by the two brigades withdrawn for rest and for special training. On the right, 45 Brigade was to attack with two battalions forward: on the right the 11th Battalion Argyll and Sutherland Highlanders (Princess Louise's) (11/A&SH) and on the left the 13th Battalion The Royal Scots (13/Royal Scots). In support were the 6/7th Battalion Royal Scots Fusiliers (6/7th RSF) and the 6/Camerons.

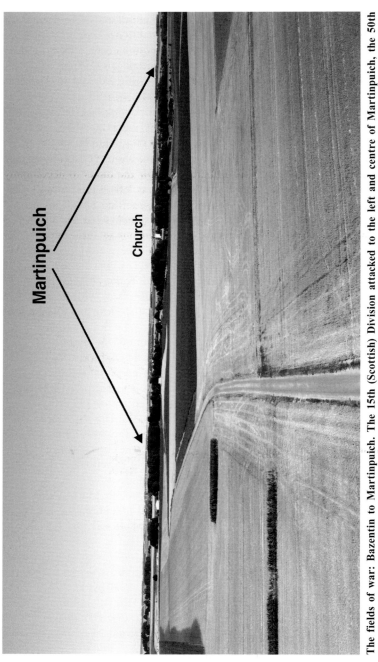

Martinpuich

Church

The fields of war: Bazentin to Martinpuich. The 15th (Scottish) Division attacked to the left and centre of Martinpuich, the 50th (Northumbrian) Division its southern portion on the right and the ground to the right of that area. (*Author*)

On the Division's left, 46 Brigade had three battalions forward: the right battalion was the 10th Cameronians (Scottish Rifles) (10/CSR), in the centre the 7/8th King's Own Scottish Borderers (7/8th KOSB) and on the left was the 10/11th Highland Light Infantry Regiment (10/11th HLI); The 12/HLI were in support. The Division's third brigade, 44 Brigade, was in reserve in the nearby village of Contalmaison.

Four tanks had been allotted to the Division. This was a new weapon and so secrecy and surprise were paramount, the exhaust noise of their arrival at the front being drowned out by aeroplanes flying over the enemy's trenches. The infantry was to advance under a covering barrage at the rate of fifty yards per minute; to allow the tanks to accompany them safely, a lane a hundred yards wide was left in the barrage plan. During the night of 14–15 September the assaulting battalions moved into position into Liver, Ham, and Bacon trenches, to the southwest of the village. The attack was to be carried out in three phases, the

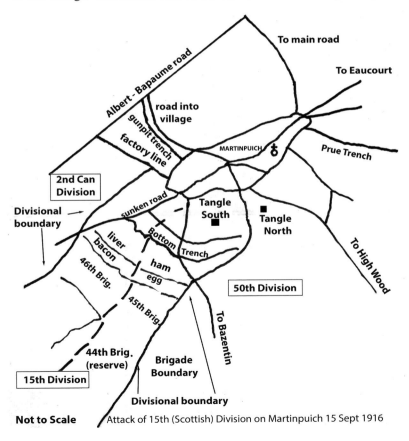

Attack of 15th (Scottish) Division on Martinpuich 15 Sept 1916

final objective for the day being the southern portion of Martinpuich. However, if any opportunity for further progress was to appear, this opportunity was to be grabbed. The Division's attack began at 6.20 am on 15 September 1916, the day cloudy but without rain.

The first objective of 46 Brigade, on the Division's left, was the Sunken Road (one of many 'Sunken Roads' on the Western Front) leading out of Martinpuich, which lay at an angle of roughly 45 degrees to the start line. The two battalions, 10/11th HLI and 7/8th KOSB, almost as soon as they went over the top, had to alter their direction to the left to attack this objective. This order for the sharp turn was received just prior to the attack and so there was no opportunity to practise it. It simply had to be successful on the day and, fortunately, indeed it was, perfectly executed. Twenty-five minutes after the attack commenced 46 Brigade had successfully captured both Tangle and Bottom trenches, along with the Sunken Road. They could now move on to their final objective. Many surprised Germans surrendered and were taken prisoner and Factory Lane, the final objective, was reached shortly afterwards. There the 10/11th HLI met up with their left flank neighbours from the 2nd Canadian Division of the Reserve Army.

On the right 45 Brigade also met with great success and shortly after 7.00 am they reached their final objective. The Brigade deployed 11/A&SH and 13/Royal Scots in front, with the 6/Cameron Highlanders in support. The 8th Battalion York and Lancaster (8/York & Lancs), who were attached from the 23rd Division, and the 6/7th RSF were in reserve. The attack met with no great opposition and The Cutting, The Tangle South, and Tangle Trench were all captured with relative ease, several prisoners being returned to the British rear.

The Germans for their part recognised the successful effect of the British bombardment. However, Generalleutnant von Stetten, commander II Bavarian Corps, in reflecting on the events of the Offensive when writing to his divisional commanders (it went higher up the command chain, of course, as well), detected worrying signs. He felt that there was more to the loss of Martinpuich and Flers than just the success of the British bombardment or even the tactics that had been adopted. In his opinion there were several major German weaknesses in the defensive arrangements. He felt that too many troops protected themselves from the British artillery and actually stopped fighting; the men themselves felt that to fire their weapons risked betraying their current position. Far more significant than this lack of shooting and the frequent failures of machine guns, von Stetten was of the opinion that there was a lack of willpower and a lack of courage to do battle. The evidence for this lay in the perceived fact that men simply surrendered and accepted the fate of being captured. In his damning conclusion and certainly without mincing his words, von Stetten stated that to fall unwounded into the hands of the enemy was shameful and left an enduring stain on a soldier's character. Strong words indeed. It was to be a frequent refrain from these commanders over these final months of the offensive; but if Allied soldiers had it bad at this time (as they certainly did) one has also to appreciate how very tough the conditions were for their opposite numbers, living under almost incessant fire, subjected to Allied air superiority (at least until about this time), undermanned, short of reliefs and rations – so far more impressive and, indeed, to the point, was the power of endurance of the majority of the German army fighting on the Somme.

Final objectives having been gained, the work of consolidation now began by both brigades. The line at this point was from Tangle South along Tangle Trench, the southern portion of Martinpuich to the Factory Lane, where the 10/11th HLI had met with the 2nd Canadian Division. On the right 45 Brigade were now in communication with the left of the neighbouring 50th Division, which was progressing towards Tangle North and Prue Trench. In accordance with the order to push on if possible, patrols were sent into Martinpuich at 9.20 am. These captured many prisoners, including several officers in a battalion headquarters. The patrols penetrated right through the village, returning an hour later with the news that the Germans had retired to a ridge about 600 yards east of the village. Patrols around the north side of the village reached Gunpit Trench, where they captured thirteen prisoners, six of whom were officers: they would also have witnessed a scene of utter carnage in the nearby sunken road, a bloodied jumble of men, guns, gun carriages and horses, all blasted to smithereens.

Four of the precious tanks had been allocated to assist in the assault, but only two materialised. One machine broke down on its way to its start line; the other did not cross the British front line until after the infantry had started and even then its assistance must be seen as very limited. Because of the difficult ground conditions, it only eventually reached the south-west corner of Martinpuich after 46 Brigade had taken its final objective. Nevertheless, it silenced several machine guns and eliminated the threat from some dugouts on the south western outskirts of the village before returning for petrol. Early that evening the tank was seen returning to Martinpuich but by this time the village had been captured.

Until now British casualties had not been heavy. However, German artillery and machine-gun fire now became ever more intense, with the inevitable result that losses increased. At noon, on learning that Martinpuich as far as the church, situated in the main street, was clear of the enemy, Major General McCracken, the Division's GOC (General Officer Commanding), ordered 45 and 46 Brigades to push forward, take the rest of the village, and establish a line of posts north of it west of the Martinpuich-Eaucourt l'Abbaye road and to connect with the right of the neighbouring 2nd Canadian Division on their left. This further attack started at about 3.00 pm and an hour later the whole of Martinpuich had been captured. On the left 46 Brigade met with practically no opposition and occupied that part of Push Alley allotted to it. On the right 45 Brigade swept through the north-east portion of the village, reached the hill on the far side and, after some bombing, forced the remainder of the Germans to surrender. 189 prisoners were taken, along with an enormous amount of ammunition and other materials that were discovered in the village. Amongst the German prisoners were officers and men of the 17th Bavarians, the 133rd Reserve, the 211th Reserve Regiments and of the 40th Field Artillery Reserve Regiment. A field gun battery and a howitzer were also captured.

During the night of the 15–16 September the work of consolidation went on, including the digging of a trench connecting the new line north of Martinpuich with Prue Trench. Apart from two futile and weak German counterattacks delivered early in the morning of the 16th, the Germans made no attempt to regain the ground given up. Martinpuich had been captured and held so that now the thoughts of the British command could be directed to pressing on northwards in this sector and consider, for example, the capture of Eaucourt l'Abbaye, Le Sars and the Butte de Warlencourt.

The 15th (Scottish) Division's history proudly stated that it would be difficult to find a better conceived and better executed operation than that of its attack on 15 September. Casualties were deemed not excessive, 'not excessive' amounting to 221 killed, 1282 wounded and 351 missing, a total of 1854, on 15 and 16 September. Prisoners numbered between 600 and 700, belonging to several regiments. In addition to the vast store of material taken in Martinpuich, numerous weapons fell into the possession of the division. On 18 September the 23rd Division commenced taking over the line from the 15th Division, which suffered 6732 casualties for August and September. It had been in the line for six weeks without relief. The same day Rawlinson sent a telegram to Major General McCracken, which he passed on to all ranks.

'From G.O.C. Fourth Army to G.O.C. Fifteenth (Scottish) Division Please convey to my old friends in the Fifteenth Division my congratulations on their splendid performance the day before yesterday. To have captured Martinpuich after having been a month in the line is a very fine performance, and I greatly appreciate their gallantry and vigorous fighting spirit.'

The relief was completed by noon on the 19th; divisional headquarters were established at Baizieux, some ten kilometres west of Albert.

The 50th (Northumbrian) Division.
It will be recalled that III Corps' 50th Division was also to attack on 15 September, the 47th (2/London) Division on their right and, as has just been described, the 15th Division on their left. Their assault was also to be made in three bounds: with 149 Brigade on the right and 150 Brigade on the left, with 151 Brigade in reserve.

The Division's first objective was Hook Trench from the north-west of High Wood to the south-east of Martinpuich; the second objective was Martin Trench, the Bow and a portion of the Starfish Line; and the third and final objectives were Prue Trench and the left of the Starfish Line. Orders were issued from 149 Brigade Headquarters to the 4th Northumberland Fusiliers (4/NF) and 7/NF to form the right and left first wave of the Brigade; the 6/NF were to be in support and 5/NF in brigade reserve. The attack was to be delivered from two lines of assembly trenches connecting to the north of Clarke's Trench.

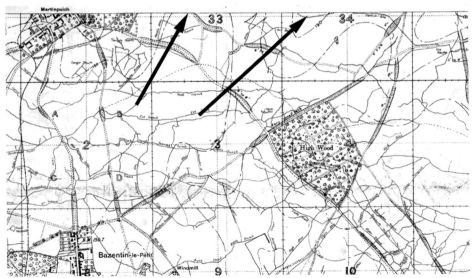

The area over which the 50th (Northumbrian) Division attacked on 15 September 1916. (*Author*)

17

150 Brigade on the left was to attack with three battalions in the front line and one battalion in reserve: 1/4th East Yorkshire (1/4 East Yorks) on the right, the 4th Alexandra, Princess of Wales's Own (The Yorkshire Regiment), the 4th Green Howards (4/Green Howards) in the centre and 5/Green Howards on the left, whilst 5/DLI were in reserve in front of the remnants of the village of Bazentin-le-Petit. The assembly positions for the attacking troops were Eye and Swansea Trenches.

The men of the 50th Division were, however, to commence their attack well forward of those of their neighbouring divisions on both their flanks. It was hoped that a quick advance would help the progress of their neighbours; but there was still a strong German presence in High Wood who had shown no inclination to be willing to withdraw from it over the last two months. Both flanks of the 50th Division were, therefore, in a most dangerous situation. Those in command had to decide whether to delay their attack until the flanking divisions came up alongside or whether to take the risk of heavy losses and start at zero hour in order to help the other two divisions progress by threatening to surround the enemy in High Wood and Martinpuich. The latter option was chosen.

At 6.10 am two tanks were seen approaching in the rear and to the left of 149 Brigade. Eight minutes later they reached and heaved themselves over the assembly trenches of the 7/NF and started off across No Man's Land towards the enemy's trenches. The divisional history states that the Germans had received warning of the use of these tanks; nevertheless, when they appeared, they certainly produced panic. Actually, at this stage the Germans had only the very dimmest idea of what these machines might be; indeed, some of the sketches produced after the tanks had been in action are quite extraordinarily inaccurate. In short, the Germans had no idea of the reality of what was coming their way. The records of Bavarian Regiment 17 show that the appearance of the two tanks was a surprise. Signals went up from the enemy's front line, and numbers of Germans ran from their trenches back towards their second line. Minutes later the expected enemy barrage fell but, as the 7/NF's War Diary states, *our men got away before a heavy fire was opened on them.*

At 6.20 am the divisional barrage fell, the attack started and the 4th and 7/NF of 149 Brigade, and the 4/East Yorks, 4th and 5/Green Howards of 150 Brigade, advanced in good order and close up to the screen of fire. They quickly gained the first objective and Hook Trench was entered at around 7.00 am. At the north-western corner of High Wood, the Germans had a very strongly defended position that provided a superb overview of the whole of the ground held by the 50th Division. This strong point, which contained numerous machine guns, had been unsuccessfully attacked on a multitude of occasions before the Division took over the line and, as a result, no sooner had 149 Brigade begun to dig in on the line of the first objective at Hook Trench when devastating machine-gun and rifle fire was opened on the 4th and 7/NF, who were on the right of the attack. It was obvious to 149 Brigade that the 47th (2/London) Division were struggling at High Wood and that the assistance of the 50th Division was going to be necessary.

The advance of the 50th Division to its second objective, which included Martin Trench, was not scheduled to begin until 7.20 am, so the men occupying the new line had to make every attempt to shelter from the devastating fire coming from their right. The Londoners had, as feared, not taken High Wood, as the left-hand brigade of that division had been held up. It was imperative, therefore, for 149 Brigade to push on and outflank the enemy holding out in the wood, thus forcing the Germans to evacuate their stronghold or be encircled and captured. At 7.20 am both 149 and 150 Brigades advanced and successfully captured the second objective, consisting of the Starfish Line, The Bow and Martin Trench but, as was anticipated, the enemy's fire from both flanks caused very heavy casualties amongst the attacking troops. The 4/NF of 149 Brigade, unsupported on their right by the 47th Division, were, however, driven back to Hook Trench. This trench and Bethel Sap were strengthened and made secure and now both the 5/NF and 6/NF, who had been in support, were in the line and fully involved in the struggle.

At 8.10 am, forty minutes after the attack on the second objective commenced, the 4/NF were ordered to help the Londoners by bombing towards the wood from which Germans were now emerging to counterattack. The 5/NF and 6/NF were also ordered to support the attack and soon after 10.00 am the 7/NF were reported to be in the sunken road south of The Bow. Losses were heavy and confused fighting took place on the right, north west, of the wood. After a tortuous struggle the wood – or what little was left of it – ultimately fell in the early afternoon.

The two attached tanks went forward in advance of the infantry and were of considerable help. One machine reached the first objective and enfiladed the trench, inflicting casualties; however, it was hit by two shells in quick succession, though this did not prevent the crew from salvaging their guns and joining the infantry. The other tank had German infantry fleeing before it and reached the vicinity of the third objective, accounting for three German machine guns on the eastern outskirts of Martinpuich. It eventually returned to its start line, having suffered some minor damage, in order to replenish its petrol.

150 Brigade's three first wave attacking battalions were to go all the way through to the final objective, supported by the 5/DLI. The first

objective was taken without difficulty before 7.00 am, which saw many Germans surrendering and running towards the British front line. The second objective was taken minutes before 8.00 am and, two hours later, the third objective was reported taken. However, the success was not permanent, as on the right the 4/East Yorks, its flank in the air, was obliged to withdraw to Martin Trench. Further to the left, the Starfish Line was held near its junction with Martin Alley. The 7/NF, on the right of the East Yorkshires, however, had not advanced in line with the latter and, although Martin Alley and Martin Trench were in the hands of 150 Brigade, no further advance could take place to the Starfish Line until 149 Brigade had advanced.

The 7/NF gave various interesting and some unexpected reasons for their delay in advancing. It was noted that Hook Trench lay along the top of a ridge but the second and third objectives were in a valley beyond and nothing could be seen of them from the assembly trenches. The battalion was, therefore, moving on compass bearings. Touch had been lost with the East Yorkshires between the first and second objectives. When near the second objective the advancing infantry had to halt as the British barrage was holding them up. Several attempts were made to get forward, but losses were so high from accidental (what is popularly known these days as 'friendly') fire that the remainder of the battalion was forced to wait until it lifted. There was another difficulty, rarely associated with fighting on the Somme: the ground was dry and had already been lambasted by constant bombardments, so the Fusiliers had found themselves screened by a veil of dust and smoke hanging over their advance. Eventually the 7/Northumberland Fusiliers reached the sunken road just south of The Bow, where they captured about thirty men of a *minenwerfer* (mortar) battery, killing several others and seizing four trench mortars. An officer of the Battalion, Captain F Buckley, recorded an amusing incident:

'The prisoners, more numerous than us, were sent to the rear in charge of Private Martin, a diminutive signaller. He caused much consternation among his flock by deftly severing their trouser buttons before the journey began. It made an imposing procession – the prisoners with their hands deep in their pockets followed by Private Martin smoking an enormous souvenir cigar and mumbling "hoh way, you blinking beggars".' [One feels, somehow, that Private Martin's choice of words were originally rather earthier, but possibly were felt not suitable for readers of a delicate disposition.]

At 10.00 am on the 15th, 150 Brigade reported the capture of its final objective. The divisional front now ran in a south-easterly direction from Martinpuich to High Wood. It is obvious that 149 Brigade met with the greatest opposition and had the most difficult task, the gap on its right flank uncovering the whole of the Brigade's attack. The Divisional narrative concluded that both brigades lost very heavily and became considerably disorganised, especially 149 Brigade; however, by splendid dash and gallantry, the brigades enabled both High Wood and Martinpuich to be captured. The 47th Division, on the division's right, lost very heavily at High Wood before the enemy finally withdrew and the surviving remnants surrendered at about 1 pm; the 15th Division occupied Martinpuich just before 10 am without difficulty, thanks to the co-operation of the 50th Division.

Haig's Somme despatches were considered unfair by the 50th Division as its members felt they were not given due credit for the assistance given to their fellow divisions in III Corps during the attacks. In the despatches the 47th Division is praised for the capture of High Wood but those men of the 50th 'in the know' felt that its capture was largely due to the decision of their GOC, Major General Perceval Wilkinson, not to wait until the two flanking divisions came up into line with him but to attack straight away, with the intention of making easier the capture of both High Wood and Martinpuich.

The prize: The ramshackle remnants of Martinpuich, now in British hands.
(***Fonds des albums Valois** – **Pas de Calais***)

During the afternoon of 16 September 149 Brigade was placed in divisional reserve and gradually battalions were withdrawn to the relative safety of nearby Mametz Wood; however, it was nearly midnight before the last of them reached their destination. It is worth considering the scene when they came out of the line and made their way the few kilometres or more back to a not particularly safe (at least from longer range artillery) support area. The ground they crossed would have been ravaged to a degree that we simply cannot imagine, shell torn, reeking of battle, largely featureless; infantry would not have had priority in the use of any half decent surfaces; they faced the prospect of being hit by German shells; they would have been very tired and, if elated at success, sobered by its price; and when they got to their 'rest' area they would have been stumbling around for the most part in the dark. At least there was some comfort from the fact that the 16th was a fine, sunny day.

The losses sustained by each battalion of the brigade from 14 to 16 September 1916 were:

4/Northumberland Fusiliers: seventeen officers killed or wounded; other ranks, 110 killed, 229 wounded, 143 missing. Total 499.

5/Northumberland Fusiliers: five officers wounded; other ranks, ten killed, fifty-four wounded and eight missing. Total seventy-seven.

6/Northumberland Fusiliers: one officer killed, eight officers wounded; other ranks, 279 killed, wounded, or missing. Total 288.

7/Northumberland Fusiliers: three officers killed, nine officers wounded; other ranks, forty killed, 219 wounded and seventy-four missing. Total 345.

The brigade's total of infantry casualties was therefore recorded as 1209; not surprisingly, the 4th and 7th battalions of the regiment accounted for some 70% of the casualties between them, the 4th suffering the most.

The line held by the 50th Division at 2.00 pm the following day ran from the eastern end of Hook Trench (the divisional right boundary point) -The Bow – part of Crescent Alley – Martin Trench – Prue Trench and the Starfish Line – west of Crescent Valley and to Martin Alley, inclusive, on the Division's left. 151 Brigade held the line on the right and 150 Brigade the left.

On the morning of the 19th, 69 Brigade of the 23rd Division relieved 150 Brigade on the divisional left. The 4/East Yorks had already gone back to the 15 September start line, where they were duly joined by the three other battalions. Losses over these last days had been high:

casualties for the 4/East Yorks during the operations from 14 to 17 September inclusive were 250. Major AL Raimes of 5/DLI stated that, when his battalion roll call was taken on 19 September, only four officers and eighty-eight men answered to their names. These figures were to swell, however, over the following few days when men who had been slightly injured and others who had become mixed with other units during the confusion of battle returned to the battalion; in addition, others would have missed the roll call because of their duties. And, presumably, the figures only referred to those who went into action and excluded the mandatory minimum of ten percent who would have been left behind in the transport lines.

Now only 151 Brigade from the Division remained in the front line. In the early hours of 21 September it was also relieved and in turn moved back to Mametz Wood; however, 149 Brigade returned to the line as their relief. The Division's action in the battle, which commenced on 15 September, was soon to be completed. Early the following morning, 22 September, an attack saw all the remaining original objectives captured; the casualties were few as the enemy had all but completely abandoned these positions. After a week's fighting the 50th (Northumbrian) Division had reached its final objective.

The 47th (1/2nd London) Division.

The fighting for High Wood is worthy of a book in its own right; it is one of what has been described as the 'horseshoe of woods' that confronted the British after the success in this southernmost part of the British line on 1 July: from north to south they were Mametz, Bazentin, High, Delville and Trônes woods and each of them in turn provided significant problems; High and Delville woods were the most stubborn centres of resistance and High Wood, the easternmost and standing on the highest ground, the last to succumb. Although somewhat outside the scope of this book, the events at High Wood were crucial for what happened in the following weeks – and it features in the tours section as well.

The 47th (1/2nd London) Division, to give it its full name, had been in France since March 1915 and had taken part in various battles since then in French Flanders, most notably at Loos, and then spent an active time on Vimy Ridge. On 20 August 1916, the Division, reinforced over the previous months, started moving to the Somme front and became part of III Corps. Its brigades were billeted along the Albert to Amiens road in the area of the villages of Bresle, Franvillers and Lahoussoye and spent the next three weeks training for the forthcoming offensive, which included early operational methods for working with tanks, admittedly very few in number as these were. Two of the brigades

The large London Cemetery before High Wood and, to its left, is the infamous north west corner of the wood. (*Stevie Kerr*)

started rehearsing for an attack on High Wood, which stood on dominating ground that was over 150 metres above sea level – hence its name. The division's artillery was already in action at the front – it had been since mid August – and had got to know the terrain over which the Division would attack well, as they had been closely supporting the 15th Division in its gradual approach to Martinpuich, some two kilometres from High Wood.

The main route from the south into Martinpuich comes from Longueval (forever associated in Great War minds with Delville Wood) and passes the western side of High Wood. The north west corner of High Wood that borders this road is just a few hundred metres north of London Cemetery and opposite the road leading to the crossroads located at the top of the village of Bazentin-le-Petit. The 47th Division moved into the line to relieve the 1st Division in this High Wood sector in the immediate run up to the Offensive. The divisional history comments on their new line:

'But we never saw anything quite like High Wood. It had been attacked by the 7th Division on July 14th – just two months before our arrival – and had indeed on that day been entered by a party of cavalry. But it had been an insuperable obstacle to subsequent attacks, and the trench which we took over ran through the centre of it, leaving more than half still in Boche hands. As for the wood, it was a wood only in name – ragged stumps sticking out of churned-up earth, poisoned with fumes of high explosives, the whole a mass of corruption.'

The history continues:

'Outside the wood the country was a featureless wilderness. The absence of natural landmarks must always be borne in mind, for it explains what might seem to be instances of confusion and bad map-reading in the progress of the operations.'

It is certainly right that these latter comments need to be kept in mind when reflecting on operational aspects of the battle between September and mid November 1916 – indeed for many of the battlefields, for when topographical features such as woods, orchards, villages and so forth have been swept away, navigation over unfamiliar ground is far from easy, made so much worse by the prevailing conditions.

The 47th (London) Division was on the right of the 50th Division and of III Corps; its left flank neighbour was the New Zealand Division of XV Corps. The latter's dominating memorial is sited on the Switch Line and is approximately 800 metres from High Wood and a kilometre from Longueval. The 47th Division attacked on a

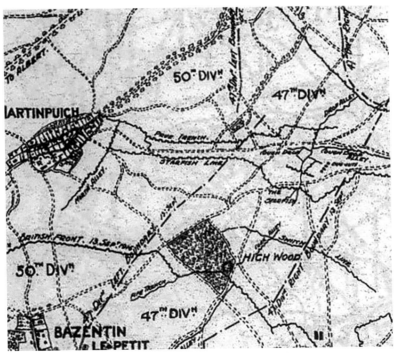

The 47th (London) Division's front on 15 September 1916.

two-brigade front, tasked with the punishing and intimidating task of capturing High Wood.

On the right was 140 Brigade. The 7th Battalion (7/Londons – the 'Shiny Seventh') was deployed outside the boundaries of the wood and would act as both left flank and the contact between the division and the New Zealanders and, indeed, as the contact between III and General du Cane's XV Corps. The 15/Londons (Civil Service Rifles) would take the eastern side of the wood. 141 Brigade, under Brigadier General McDouall, with the 17/Londons on the right and the 18/Londons on the left, had the remainder of the wood facing them along the whole of their front.

The attack had three objectives, designated on the map by coloured lines: a line clear of High Wood; the Starfish Line, down the forward slope; and lastly, on the right, the Flers Line. Here 140 Brigade were to join up with the New Zealand Division on their right before joining 141 Brigade in a communication trench, Drop Alley, from where the final objective was prolonged westwards, along Prue Trench towards Martinpuich.

III Corps was allocated eight tanks, four of which were to pass through High Wood. The front lines in High Wood were too close to permit a close support artillery bombardment and so it was hoped that the tanks would come into their own and clear the wood. There was (justifiable) doubt surrounding the capability of this innovatory weapon in such difficult ground conditions; of course these were bad everywhere on the Somme front, but to the perils of shell holes and slippery chalk-mud were the mangled remains of trees and, most of all, nature's tank trap, tree stumps. It certainly would have been preferred in certain quarters if the route taken by the tanks was kept to the wood's perimeters: but then where would be the flexible fire support needed for the battalions attacking into the wood?

As elsewhere along the Offensive's front, zero hour was at 6.20 am and the troops attacking High Wood were at once engaged in very heavy fighting. The four tanks accompanied the attack but, as forecast and feared, could make almost no headway over the broken tree-stumps and horrendous ground conditions; one managed to cross the German front line and was able to enfilade the support line but was then put out of action. The others could not manage the wood itself and went for more open ground (though one had already ditched in No Man's Land), one ditched in a shell hole and one lost direction and ended up in the British front line and even fired at its own troops. This might sound ridiculous, but I would urge someone to try and drive one of these early tanks and not get lost and disoriented, given an extremely limited view, over featureless and ravaged terrain, being fired at, with fragments of metal rattling around the tank, in a metal box with an engine making a horrendous din and creating ghastly, noxious fumes, the whole not helped by the rattle of discharging weapons in a confined space.

During the morning five battalions were deployed in the wood and casualties were very heavy; the wood might have been shattered but close quarter fighting in woods is always demanding – amongst other things, effective command and control is very difficult (military wisdom was and is to by-pass woods and take them by encirclement) and, though there might not have been much of a wood left by mid September, High Wood was no exception.

On the Division's left the 50th Division went forward and took its second objective; but, with their right flank exposed, due to the lack of progress made by 141 Brigade, they could not hold their ground. The delay at High Wood, where so many battalions had been involved in the fighting, saw revised orders being issued just over four hours after the attack had started. At 10.30 am the second objective, the Starfish Line, was promoted to the main objective and the key position to be consolidated. After a temporary withdrawal of men (or at least as best as possible) and a further intensive bombardment of High Wood, the Germans began to surrender; by around 1.00 pm the wood was deemed to be clear of the enemy. Naturally, once this was apparent the German guns reacted with great fury and heavily shelled the captured ground – ground which, of course, the Germans knew very well after two years of occupation.

The Starfish Line, 700 yards to the north, still had to be captured. With 142 Brigade in reserve and called into action at 3.30 pm, the 21/Londons and 24/Londons attacked this objective at around 6.00 pm. On the right the 21/Londons attacked the Starfish Line, and captured Starfish Redoubt itself, but their attempt to progress further failed. The 24/Londons, attacking from the wood, met such heavy fire that they did not get to the Starfish Line but dug themselves in about 200 yards in front of the first objective of 141 Brigade; the night was spent consolidating the ground held. Casualties had been horrendous. The 21/Londons had only two officers and sixty other ranks left unwounded out of the seventeen officers and 550 other ranks who had gone into the attack. When darkness fell, the Division held no organised positions forward of their first objectives except on the extreme right, where the 6/Londons were in touch with the New Zealanders to their right. The wood had been cleared – in itself something of a triumph – but their objectives had been far from achieved. By 21 September, the division was relieved and moved to the Baizieux area, well west of Albert.

The heavy losses incurred in the capture of High Wood and the consequent delays in the carrying out of the attack by the 47th Division and by the 50th Division on its left, have sometimes been seen as a result of the decisions taken regarding the use of the tanks in the 47th Division's area. The tanks had been largely successful in the capture of nearby Flers; but here the tanks could not move through the wood, in large measure owing to the insurmountable nature of the obstacles inside it. This decision was taken despite opposition and urgent representations, more than once expressed to higher command by the Divisional GOC (Major General Sir Charles Barter) after he had personally reconnoitred High Wood. Had the tanks been

Laying telephone wires in the former No Man's Land near High Wood in October 1916. (*Fonds des albums Valois* – Pas de Calais)

placed on the outside of the wood, as urged by Sir Charles, they could have materially helped the attackers in the wood, assuming that they survived the other perils that faced them. Their ineffectiveness was possibly decisive; for the Division had to assault without a covering barrage, as previously mentioned, because of the proximity of the opposing lines and so were the cause of the infantry having to attack the wood without artillery assistance other than mortars (which, in fact, performed well). A whole brigade was, in the event, effectively put out of action early on in the attack, not to mention the consequent confusion, and the ripple effect upset the advance of the division on the left, which was completely disrupted – and thereby the potential for success of the whole of the opening stage of the offensive. It was also to cost Barter his job!

Haig had decided to risk the use of the new, surprisingly still almost unknown to the Germans, weapon of the tank. Many have argued that this was to throw away the potential of the first use of the tank in an attempt to enhance further the possibility of decisive action on the Somme. The jury is out on how effective they might have been even if there had been many of them and it is uncertain when – and where – might have been the best possibility to use them first.

Of the thirty-two tanks that reached the starting point on 15 September, nine advanced with the infantry, nine failed to catch or keep up with the infantry but did assist in clearing captured ground, nine broke down and five were ditched in the craters of the battlefield. The first nine rendered useful aid, especially in capturing close by Flers, but the overall performance of the tanks was not outstanding, whilst the cost of giving up the considerable element of surprise was a high price for an attempt to redeem what could be seen as a failure of the overall Somme offensive.

The results of the attack of 15 September for the Fourth Army on its front fell far short of the desired achievement. High Wood, Martinpuich and nearby Flers had been taken and were successes; however, the adjoining villages of Morval and Lesboeufs, for example, were still in German hands and were not to fall for another ten days. It was determined that the attack was to continue, the intention, even in mid-September, according to the Official History, 'to enable the Cavalry Corps to push through to its objectives and complete the enemy's defeat'.

The first task now facing III Corps was to capture the third objective along its entire front, then to push forward its right and, in two stages, to reach Eaucourt l'Abbaye and the spur south west of it. This was a hard enough task without, as will be seen, the troops having to battle through slime, mud and the generally abysmal conditions. It was going to be two weeks before the hamlet of Eaucourt l'Abbaye fell.

A conference was held at Army headquarters on 17 September. Here Rawlinson revealed a worrying shortage of 18-pound ammunition; over 600,000 rounds had been fired since 12 September. Stocks had been depleted by over two-thirds in a week. The situation as regards the supply of howitzer and ammunition of all other calibres was satisfactory, but the Army commander said that in general artillery expenditure must be 'eased down' and devoted to further objectives. Rawlinson criticised the tendency 'to use troops up too quickly' and warned corps commanders that he saw no prospect of further reinforcements before the 21st.

The next day, the 18th, a new enemy appeared from the skies: following a wet night, rain fell nearly throughout the following day and made it difficult, often impossible, for wheeled vehicles, including guns, to move across country. Indeed, there was not enough labour or material for work to be carried out on the already damaged and limited network of tracks and roads, themselves essentially comprised of chalk beds, which in places dissolved into deep slime. The problems of men living in these conditions, let alone fighting in them, became increasingly pressing as the weeks passed by, an issue that the infantry of both sides just had to endure. As September ended, the men now began to see the mud as their chief enemy.

The Germans, therefore, had their own problems: the days of copious manpower were rapidly disappearing for them as well, legions of men having been lost at Verdun and on the Somme. What was their reaction following the fall of places such as Martinpuich? Like the other armies, they also were on a learning curve, especially as regards the essential resource, men.

The changes had begun to ring at command level in the German army with Erich von Falkenhayn's dismissal: he had been adamant from day one of the Somme offensive that no ground should be given up. His replacements made the conservation of manpower a major priority and saw no point in relentless, obviously badly planned and executed, counter attacks. These piecemeal efforts often came to nothing, especially now that the old front line of 1 July was some distance off to the west of the line by September. Before there had been all sorts of tactical operations to deal with limited breakthroughs: now there was not the time nor the manpower to engage in such luxuries, whilst many of the reinforcements that Hindenburg and Ludendorff ordered into the Somme area had little or no experience of the battlefield.

At the end of a tour of duty in the Martinpuich sector in September, General von Petersdorff, commanding the 50th Reserve Division noted

'It is the duty of all commanders to determine how they can meet the demands of the battle with as little commitment of infantry as possible. The fewer the men deployed into areas under enemy artillery fire the better and the lower the casualties will be. The proof of this is shown by the fact that newly deployed companies have a battle strength of 160 men or more. After a few days this reduces to a hundred men or fewer. The size of the sector is unchanged, and yet it is held just as successfully as it was on the day of deployment. The throwing in [piecemeal] of battalions and regiments is particularly detrimental. Passing through rear areas behind the battle front often kilometres deep and that are covered by artillery fire demands proper consideration, frequently even reconnaissance. It must never be forgotten that the battle does not begin for the infantry only once they arrive in the trenches. Negotiating the enemy artillery fire [during the approach march] is already a part of the battle – and not the easiest.'

The Battle of Flers-Courcelette in III Corps' sector had seen Martinpuich taken relatively easily by the 15th Division. The performance of the 50th Division on their right had been hampered by the prolonged fighting at High Wood, especially its north western corner; the wood was only eventually secured some seven hours after the attack had started. The decision to use the tanks through the wood itself was too much for their limited and primitive capabilities. It is interesting to speculate as to the outcome if they had been deployed in the open, on the perimeter of the wood. This might have meant that it would have fallen more quickly, though it also has to be acknowledged that the ground all around High Wood had been particularly badly affected and churned up by the almost incessant stream of shells that had struck it over eight or nine weeks, with all the consequences that would have on the movement of the tanks. In the end, finally, this dominant wood, on its distinctive concave summit, had fallen; but, in Rawlinson's words, the troops had been used up too quickly. The 50th Division took a week to secure all of its objectives for 15 September, whilst the 47th Division had barely got beyond their first objective. They were able to fight on; but the hefty cost of continuing the fight was to be over 4500 casualties of all ranks for four days' fighting.

Chapter Three

Early October: Eaucourt l'Abbaye is taken

The Battle of Flers-Courcelette officially lasted one week, 15–22 September 1916. The result on the ground was that another section of Somme ground had fallen into Allied hands, just two years after it had been seized by the Germans in the latter stages of the war of movement in 1914. There had been no breakthrough. It was time for a brief respite and a reassessment. The attention of Reserve Army, north of the Bapaume road, was switched to preparations for the Battle of Thiepval Ridge, 26–30 September; and for Fourth Army, to the south, for the Battle of Morval, 25–28 September.

Thus by the end of the month, in the area east of the Albert to Bapaume road, the villages of Martinpuich, Flers, Gueudecourt, Morval, Lesboeufs and Combles (or at least their devastated ruins) had been captured. In a letter from GHQ dated 29 September, Fourth Army was instructed

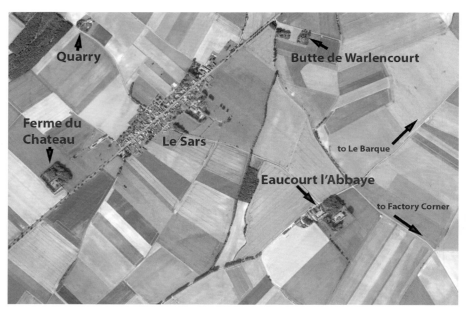

Overview of Eaucourt l'Abbaye and Le Sars area.

to begin preparations for the next big attack: the offensive process was to start again. The objectives this time including the ridge beyond the Thilloy-Warlencourt valley and Loupart Wood, located just to the north of Warlencourt. Every effort was to be made to start this attack by 12 October and until that date the Army was instructed to push northward to the near (ie southern) side of the Thilloy-Warlencourt valley, where the hamlet of Eaucourt l'Abbaye (l'Abbaye d'Eaucourt) is situated, about a kilometre from Le Sars.

Today Eaucourt l'Abbaye is a complex of farm buildings, easily reached by the road leading south east from the main crossroads in

The Abbot of Eaucourt is amongst those named in a summary of the meetings of the Estates of Artois, 1765. (*Bibliothèque nationale de France*)

Le Sars; this road ultimately joins the D10 (leading to Bapaume) at the infamous Somme battlefield site of Factory Corner, two kilometres further on. Eaucourt over the centuries has been called Aiulcurtis, Aecurtis and Yaucourt, before settling on the current name of Eaucourt from the middle of the eighteenth century. It was at the start of the twelfth century that the 'abbaye' was established at the edge of Eaucourt and in the middle of woods – long since gone. As much else in this area, it was vulnerable to the incessant border wars between France and Spain (via the latter's territories in Flanders and Artois) and it was sacked in 1651. The monastery was dissolved in 1790, soon after the French Revolution of a year earlier; and in due course the abbey's buildings were solved off as state property.

In 1916 the site comprised two large farms, in the same enclosure, built on the site of a low-lying area at the point where a short valley from the direction of High Wood turns at a right angle north-west towards the main Albert-Bapaume road. Eaucourt l'Abbaye, therefore, was overlooked by higher ground on all sides except from the north-west. The Germans held Eaucourt and it was significantly fortified. Although a small place (and small meant nothing as regards its importance or tactical significance on the Somme – one only has to think of the battering and repeated attacks that Mouquet Farm endured and resisted), this hamlet would not be any walkover when it came to attacking it.

The expression 'straightening the line' was well worn during the war and not one that was well received by those who did the straightening. There was, of course, a logic behind it; but this did not take away the feeling that the price to be paid in many such instances was quite disproportionate to the benefit accrued. On 28 September an order was issued that a major effort was to be made for just such an exercise, to take place three days later, which included the capture of

The entrance to Eaucourt l'Abbaye at the time of the war. (*Author*)

Eaucourt l'Abbaye and of the two Flers lines as far as Le Sars; it would involve an attack along the whole of III Corps' front. Progress towards this goal had already been made by the infantry on 27 September but there remained a lot to do to achieve the capture of Eaucourt. As was the case in the taking of Martinpuich over two weeks earlier, the 47th and the 50th Divisions were to be pivotal in the capture of Eaucourt l'Abbaye and its surrounds.

Following the attack on High Wood on 15 September, six days later the three brigades of the 47th Division were located at Hénencourt,

Modern day l'Abbaye d'Eaucourt (Eaucourt l'Abbaye), approaching from the Le Sars road. This was the troublesome north western side in the 1916 fighting. (*Author*)

34

Charles St. Leger Barter, born in 1857, was the son of the Rev JT Barter of Bercham, County Cork. He was commissioned in the 105th Foot (later 2nd Battalion King's Own Yorkshire Light Infantry) on 1 September 1875. Passing out from Sandhurst in 1883, he saw active service in the Ashanti Expedition (1895–6), the Tirah Campaign (1897) and the South African War (1899–1901), during which he was wounded. He completed a four-year tour in command of the Poona Brigade in India in June 1913. Just over a year later, Barter, at the age

Major General Charles St. Leger Barter (*The Great War Magazine, Part 95*)

of 57, returned to the army. On 5 September 1914 he was appointed GOC of the 47th (1/2nd London) Division TF in succession to Major-General C. Monro. Paradoxically, the capture of High Wood all but terminated Barter's military career. Soon after the battle, with next to no notice, he was charged with wasting men and was sacked from his command. It is now felt that he was made a scapegoat by the commander of III Corps, Lieutenant General Sir William Pulteney, who had repeatedly refused to listen to Barter's reasoned objections to III Corps' plan of attack based on sending tanks into the wood. Tank commanders were horrified by the idea, arguing that the shattered tree stumps everywhere in the wood made it impassable to tanks. After making a personal visit to the area with the GOC of 141 Brigade, Brigadier General Robert McDouall, Barter agreed with them. He asked III Corps to allow him to withdraw his infantry from their forward positions, close to the German front line, so that a proper artillery barrage could proceed the infantry attack, and allow him to send the tanks round the flanks of the wood to pinch it out. This refusal to agree to a very sensible plan had predictable consequences for the 47th Division, which lost very heavily in the attack, with the tanks making no or minimal impact. Barter devoted the rest of his life to an unsuccessful attempt to obtain an inquiry into his dismissal; however, his subsequent treatment, including being awarded a KCMG in 1918 and promotion to lieutenant general, suggest a tacit recognition of his unfair treatment. Surviving members of the Division seem not to have laid the blame for the

Senior officers at the dedication of the 47th Division's Memorial in Martinpuich. (*Author*)

casualties of High Wood on Barter, who was welcomed at post-war divisional reunions and called upon to unveil many of the division's composite units' war memorials. Barter was not, however, on the committee formed in 1923 to consider war memorials in the Martinpuich area: they were finalized as a stone cross erected on the western edge of High Wood and the gateway and children's play area of the school in Martinpuich. He was a co-signatory, with three others, of a letter to *The Times* asking for donations to offset the costs which, according to the letter, were not expected to exceed £1000. Barter is also not mentioned in the Special Order of the Day of Past and Present Officers of the 47th (London) Division present at the unveiling ceremonies that took place on 15 September 1925. Lieutenant General Sir George Gorringe, who took over the Division a few days after Barter's dismissal, was present. Barter retired from the army on 20 December 1918 and died in 1931.

Bresle, and Millencourt, all around eight to ten kilometres due west of Albert. The division's fighting strength had been partially replenished following its sterling efforts at High Wood; however, it still had a net loss of nearly 1600 officers and men since that fighting and the fact was that the reinforcements were likely, for the most part, to have had no experience of combat. On 28 September the Division's GOC, Major

General Sir Charles St. L Barter KCB CVO, was sacked. He had never been a favourite of higher command and had come very close to being removed when Sir Henry Wilson was his Corps commander in early 1916. However, Barter had commanded the Division since September 1914, in the early days of training, had taken it out to France, and commanded it in French Flanders, at the Battle of Loos and at Vimy Ridge, culminating in the bloody battle for High Wood.

The new GOC, Major General Sir George F Gorringe, KCB CMG DSO, took over command from Barter after a few days' gap, during which the Division was temporarily commanded by Major General WH Greenly. The timing of the change in command was hardly conducive to the Division's morale! By dawn on the 29th, with recovery time in the relative peace of the countryside behind Albert over, 141 Brigade had taken over the line from the 1st Division. The 20/Londons made an attack on a German strong point in the Flers Line, which needed to be removed before the major thrust against Eaucourt could be carried out; this failed. Various reasons were cited, including insufficient heavy artillery, a lack of infantry and a shortage of bombs. The position was taken the following day. It showed that the Flers Line was strongly held and the Germans still had shelters which had not been destroyed by the artillery.

The Battle of Transloy Ridge opened on 1 October, officially ending on the 18th; indeed, the fighting extended all the way up to the Ancre and involved both Fourth and Reserve Armies. Notably, Thiepval and Mouquet Farm, north of the Bapaume road, had fallen by the end of September. III Corps had its part to play.

On 1 October, two days after the Londons had arrived back at the front, the attack on Eaucourt l'Abbaye and the enemy's defences to its east and west commenced. The 47th Division was to attack with three battalions of 141 Brigade and the planned assistance of two tanks. The attacking London units, from right to left, were the 19th, 20th and 17th battalions. The 18/Londons were in support, and, farther back, the 23/Londons were also placed under the command of 141 Brigade. There is an interesting entry in the brigade war diary, noting that the men had to be given a reminder that too many soldiers had been arriving slightly injured at dressing stations without their fighting weapons. They were instructed that if they were wounded on the advance that it must be a point of honour to bring their rifles with them to the dressing station.

The two tanks had to start some distance behind the infantry for concealment; they made for the right of the divisional front, which was some 1100 metres or so ahead. They had orders to pass up the Flers trenches to Eaucourt l'Abbaye and so could not reach the village until

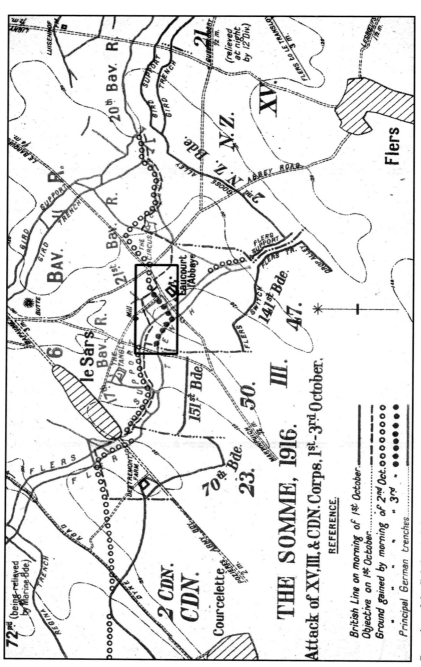

Overview of the fighting 1–3 October, showing the positions of the 47th, 50th and 23rd Divisions. Note the delay in the capture of the north western side of Eaucourt l'Abbaye, the boxed area on the map.

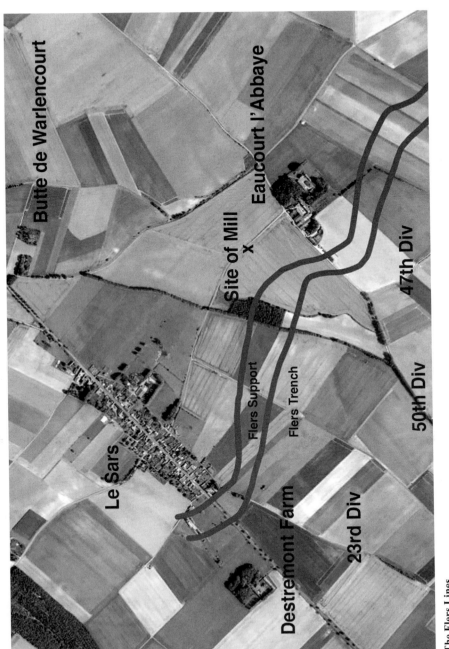

The Flers Lines.

well after zero hour. Attacking to the left of the 47th Division was the 50th Division, whose actions will be covered shortly.

As the attack commenced, the two battalions on the right entered the Flers Line without difficulty; but their further advance was held up by machine-gun fire from the west corner of the old Abbey enclosure. The 19/Londons on the right were forced to wait in shell holes fifty yards from the German positions because of accurate machine-gun fire, waiting until the tanks came up, moving right to left along the Flers Line. The tanks, it will be recalled, had been held back, with their route to the German front line in Flers Trench taking them via another former redoubt, the Cough Drop, situated between Flers and Martinpuich: their journey to the action was therefore over a total of more than a kilometre of heavily scarred battlefield.

The machines were those of Second Lieutenant HGF Bown and Lieutenant WJ Wakley. Bown had already been in action on 15 September; despite his tank being damaged, he had carried out excellent work by protecting the flank of the New Zealand Division between Longueval and High Wood, for which he was awarded the Military Cross. On that day he had commanded the male tank D8 and he was again in the same machine. Wakley had not taken part in this earlier action but his tank, numbered D16, had.

The tanks were obviously too far behind, owing to the lack of covered approaches, to be able to take part in the opening of the attack, but they were soon seen advancing on either side of the Eaucourt l'Abbaye-Flers line, continuously in action, and doing splendid work. The infantry waiting in the shell holes were soon able to rise and follow the tanks on their northerly path. D8 crossed the Flers Line and then continued over Flers Support, before turning left in the direction of Eaucourt. On the way there Bown met resistance but destroyed this with point-blank fire from his machine. In the interim, D16 drove up between the two trenches before meeting up with D8, where Bown was once more seen using his gun to good effect on the German defences around the farm enclosure. Soon after the two tanks parted company again.

On the right, where most of the enemy opposition had been swept away, the 19/Londons were able to swing to the east of the farm and link up with the New Zealanders along the Le Barque road. Their immediate colleagues on the left, the 20/Londons, poured through the remains of the farm to join up with the 19/Londons. The new position was successfully held by men under Lieutenant LW Needham, of the 20/Londons, under most difficult conditions until a complete line was established around all of Eaucourt l'Abbaye.

141st INFANTRY BRIG.D.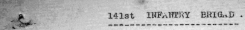

At ZERO the two "Tanks" operating with the 141st Brigade will leave their position of assembly at the ST.RFISH and proceed along the following route :-

From ST.RFISH to M.35.a.2.6. and thence up the road keeping on the Eastern side of it to M.29.b.3.0.

They will then cross the FLERS LINE and FLERS SUPPORT LINE and proceed N.F. to EAUCOURT L'ABBAYE, and will assist the infantry in clearing up the situation.

On conclusion of their task they will return and report to O.C. their Company.

L. Clemens.

Add. 2. 0.0.122.

Captain,
Brigade Major,
141st Inf.Bde.

Issued to all recipients of C.0.122 d/d 30th Sept.1916.

141 Brigade's operational orders for the two attached tanks (*National Archives*)

The 20/Londons, in their eagerness to get on, had failed, however, to ensure that the Abbey's buildings were cleared of the enemy. This was to have serious consequences. Both tanks soon became ditched in the Flers Line south-west of the farm. The two tank commanders decided that, to prevent their tanks falling into the hands of the enemy, they should set fire to their machines and withdraw. Bown's men escaped unscathed; Wakley and one of his men were wounded as they made their way back.

Without the support of the tanks, the 17/Londons on the left of the divisional attack, already brought to a halt by uncut wire and ferocious enemy machine-gun fire, found themselves in grave danger of being overrun and, when the enemy counter-attacked down both Flers Line and Flers Support, they fell back. As they did so they were then fired on by Germans emerging from the ruins of the farm and they suffered in consequence. As at High Wood, the troops on the right had gone forward and occupied their objective, but the position was compromised by an unprotected left flank. This in turn meant that the right flank of the neighbouring 50th Division in the Flers Line was open.

To resolve this critical situation, the 23/Londons was ordered to attack the Flers Line and to push on through the hamlet to join up with the 19 and 20/Londons. This operation was planned for 5.00 am the following day but, owing to a dark, wet night, the battalion did not assemble until 6.25 am, when it attacked twenty minutes later in the light of the early autumn Somme. The battle-weary battalion also found the going difficult and the advancing waves were cut down by machine-gun fire from the flank; and the battalion was withdrawn, suffering around 170 casualties. On the following day, at 3.35 pm, two companies of 18/Londons attacked up the Flers Line successfully, got through Eaucourt l'Abbaye, and completed the circuit of British troops around the small settlement.

On 4 October 140 Brigade took over the line from 141 Brigade in preparation for yet another general attack, this attack planned for 7 October. In the interim, the following day, the 6/Londons captured the ruined mill that was some 500 yards north west of Eaucourt l'Abbaye.

The significance of the capture of Eaucourt l'Abbaye and surrounds was that it enabled several of the artillery batteries to be moved forward and over High Wood ridge into this new area, where they remained for their stay on the Somme. They were able to provide close support covering fire for the gallant but ultimately unsuccessful attacks on the Butte de Warlencourt that took place over the next weeks.

The advance by the infantry of III Corps on 1 October was watched from the air above the battlefield by Major J Chammier, the commanding officer of 34 Squadron RFC. He commented:

'At 3.15 pm the steady bombardment changed into a most magnificent barrage. The timing of this was extremely good. Guns opened [fire] simultaneously, and the effect was that of many machine guns opening fire on the same order. As seen from the air the barrage appeared to be a most perfect wall of fire in which it was inconceivable that anything could live. The 47th (London) Division took more looking for than the 50th, and it was my impression at the time that they were having some difficulty in getting into formation for an attack from their forming up places, with the result that they appeared to be very late and to be some distance behind the barrage when it lifted off the German front line at Eaucourt l'Abbaye and immediately to the west of it. It was plain that here there was a good chance of failure and this actually came about, for the men had hardly advanced a couple of hundred yards, apparently, when they were seen to fall and take cover among shell-holes, being presumably held up by machine-gun and rifle fire. It was not possible to verify this owing to the extraordinary noise of the bursting shells of the barrage. The tanks were obviously too far behind, owing to lack of covered approaches, to be able to take part in the original attack, but they were soon seen advancing on either side of the Eaucourt l'Abbaye-

Flers Line, continuously in action and doing splendid work. They did not seem to be a target of much enemy shell fire. The enemy barrage appeared to open late, quite five minutes after the commencement of our own barrage, and when it came it bore no resemblance to the wall of fire which we were putting up.'

The Official History quotes Bavarian sources as saying that Eaucourt l'Abbaye was regarded as lost on the afternoon of 1 October. It is, of course, regrettable that the tanks were unable to support the 17/Londons beyond the farm, for this would have helped their neighbour, the 50th Division, in their attempt to capture Le Sars; but it is considered that the tanks did play a major role in the successful taking of Eaucourt l'Abbaye.

In due course it became apparent that the attack on 1 October could have been completely successful. The German battalion that had met the 141 Brigade attack was expecting relief that night and had left before their relief arrived (something of an indication, perhaps, of its state of morale). The Germans quickly reacted and rushed up a battalion from support to occupy the Flers Line opposite Eaucourt l'Abbaye; one tried to go east of the village but was stopped by the British barrage and the fire of the advancing infantry of 141 Brigade; the other came west of the village through the gap, and occupied their trenches just in time to meet the attack of the 23/Londons the next morning.

1 October: The 50th Division.
The 50th Division, on the left of the 47th, had as their objectives on 1 October the Flers lines to the east of Eaucourt l'Abbaye. To their left was the 23rd Division, facing the Flers lines opposite Le Sars. For anybody touring the area this is a good example of being able to view a major action: the fighting front of these three divisions as the crow flies from the Le Sars to Eaucourt l'Abbaye is approximately 1300 metres and is still largely open, agricultural ground. In the course of the fighting Lieutenant Colonel Roland BT Bradford, CO of the 9/DLI, part of 151 Brigade, 50th Division, carried out the actions that resulted in the award of the Victoria Cross for his fine leadership near Eaucourt l'Abbaye.

All preparations on the 50th Division's front were completed by dawn on 1 October, the hour of attack set for 3.15 pm. Wire cutting had begun the previous day, and during the night of the 30 September-1 October the enemy trenches were subjected to heavy shelling, the Germans' response being particularly heavy in the early morning.

Situated in the centre of the Corps' front, 151 Brigade of the 50th Division attacked with, on the right, the 6/DLI and in the centre a composite battalion of the 5th Border Regiment (5/Borders), now too

151st Inf Bde. start that attack will be carried on on 1st Oct as follows —
In the front line — in four waves. Right 6th DLI
Centre. 5th Bordrs (2 waves) 8th DLI (2 waves)
Left 5th North⁴ Fus.
In Support. Right 9th D.L.I.
Left 6th North⁴ Fus.

Bns two Battalions
The 149th Inf Bde. is in Support — On the Right 1st North Fus. On the Left. 7th North⁴ Fus.

The 150th Inf Bde. is in Reserve. — 4th East Yorks and 4th Yorks in CLARKS TRENCH.
5th Yorks and 5th D.L.I. in OG Line (S.13.8)

151 Brigade's deployment orders for the attack on 1 October.

weak in numbers, and the 8/DLI. On their left was the 5/NF, attached from 149 Brigade. The infantry was to attack in four waves, with the 9/DLI in reserve and the 4/NF in close support. The preliminary bombardment commenced at 7.00 am and continued until 3.15 pm, when it grew in intensity into a barrage. There were some casualties from shells falling short. This was the price paid for close artillery support, especially when one considers the problems the gunners faced of firing from new locations, often on unstable ground and with guns whose barrels were quite likely worn from their extensive use. The War Diary of 151 Brigade Headquarters gives a brief description of the initial assault:

'The advance was carried out in perfect order, all men moving forward at the correct time and creeping up to the barrage. Our barrage was a perfect wave of fire without any gaps.'

These remarks are fully in line with those made by Chammier, quoted earlier, who witnessed the attack from the air.

Major GE Wilkinson, the commanding officer of the 6/DLI, was wounded before the infantry attack was launched, at 2.35 pm. Lieutenant Colonel RB Bradford, commanding the 9/DLI, which was in support, asked for and was given permission to take command of the two battalions. He arrived at 6/DLI's battalion headquarters at zero and at once went up to the front line. The attack commenced at 3.15 pm but, partly on account of the failure of the 47th Division on the right and partly owing to the wire not being sufficiently cut, they were held up by machine-gun fire and suffered heavy casualties. On the right of the attack, the 6/DLI captured the German front line but could not make contact on the right flank with the Londoners, which had not succeeded in taking its first objective and Eaucourt. The enemy counter attacked and drove the Durhams from Flers Trench.

During the evening, however, the battalion again attacked and partially regained their objective. They had again captured Flers Trench on their front, though the 47th Division had still not succeeded in advancing in line with the Durhams. The latter, therefore, had to build a block in the trench, as its right flank was in the air. Meanwhile, the 5/Borders and the 8/DLI, the centre battalions, had gained both the German first (Flers Trench) and second Flers (Flers Support) lines. The War Diary of 5/Borders records their part in the battle:

'The two lines were captured before the enemy realised that we were in possession. A very small number only of the battalion on our right (6/Durham Light Infantry) reached the first objective, the result being that the composite Battalion of the 5th Border Regiment and the 8th Durham Light Infantry had a very strenuous and responsible time in clearing their right flank and forming blocks thereto. An enemy machine gun was captured on the first objective, as it was beginning to cause trouble.'

The records of the 8/DLI do not differ materially from those of the 5/Borders. The Battalion advanced in good order, *close under our barrage, which was most successful*. The smoke from bursting shells acted as a smoke screen, so that the troops took the first objective practically without a casualty. The Durhams captured about twenty-five prisoners, but the German garrisons generally are described as *retiring, running*. On the left the 5/NF reported that at 3.15 pm,

'... the whole line disappeared over ridge and was obscured by smoke of bursting shells. Our barrage opened very intense and, we afterwards heard, with excellent results. Enemy's artillery opened promptly, but the battalions had already passed their barrage zone.'

Shortly after 4.00 pm both of its assaulting companies reported the capture of their second objective, ie the second Flers Line (Flers Support), and began consolidating.

The supporting battalions also took their part in the battle. The 9/ DLI, in support of the 6/DLI, joined the fray. As a result of their efforts, a renewed assault by parts of both these battalions secured the Flers Line by about 9.30 pm, with Flers Support following some four hours later. The composite battalion and the Northumberland Fusiliers had captured both the Flers lines in the centre and on the left without much trouble, the Germans allowed no time to organise an effective resistance.

The 50th Division's task was completed before dawn on 2 October 1916, thanks to the sterling efforts of Colonel 'Boy' Bradford in driving the enemy from Flers Support to his front and by using elements of the 6 and 9/DLI to barricade and secure his right flank from the Germans, due to the failure of the 47th Division to get forward in that area.

Rain started falling at about mid-morning on 2 October, which then turned into a heavy downpour, with the earth in freshly dug trenches quickly turning to mud that clung obstinately to absolutely everything. In these conditions 149 Brigade were told to relieve the battle weary 151 Brigade; and the following day 68 Brigade of the 23rd Division took over the line, the relief not completed until the early hours of 4 October as a consequence of the horrid weather and generally torrid conditions. The 50th (Northumbrian) Division left the line with a lengthy casualty list; between 10 September to 3 October it came to 4072 all ranks.

An Eaucourt l'Abbaye Victoria Cross winner.

Lieutenant Colonel Roland Boys Bradford of the 9/Durham Light Infantry was awarded the Victoria Cross for his fine leadership at Eaucourt l'Abbaye on 1 October 1916. Bradford was presented with his medal by King George V during an open-air ceremony in Hyde Park in June 1917. The Victoria Cross citation of Lieutenant (Temporary Lieutenant Colonel) Roland Boys Bradford MC: London Gazette, 25 November 1916, states:

'For most conspicuous bravery and good leadership in attack, whereby he saved the situation on the right flank of his Brigade and of the Division. Lieutenant Colonel Bradford's battalion was in support. A leading battalion having suffered very severe casualties and the Commander wounded; its flank became dangerously exposed at close quarters to the enemy. Raked by machine-gun fire, the situation of the battalion was critical. At the request of the wounded Commander, Lieutenant Colonel Bradford asked permission to command the exposed battalion in addition to his own. Permission granted, he at once proceeded to the foremost lines. By his fearless energy under fire of all descriptions, and by skilful leadership of the two battalions, regardless of all danger, he succeeded in rallying the attack, captured and defended the objective, and so secured the flank.'

In recognition of his abilities, Roland Bradford was made temporary GOC of 186 Brigade on 10 November 1917 and promoted temporary brigadier general on 13 November at the extraordinarily young age of 25, the youngest man to hold general rank in the British army in the Great War and, indeed, in modern times. Sadly, the career of Brigadier General Bradford VC MC lasted just twenty days. During the Battle of Cambrai he was killed by a German shell splinter near Lock 7 on the Canal du Nord, about a mile from Graincourt, whilst visiting

Brigadier General Roland B Bradford's grave in Hermies Cemetery. (*Author*)

(unaccompanied) his brigade's positions. He is buried in Hermies British Cemetery (F 10), only fourteen kilometres from Bapaume and easily reached by vehicle.

His brother, Lieutenant Commander George Bradford RN, also won the Victoria Cross, for his part in the Zeebrugge Raid on St George's Day April 1918. He was killed in the action that won him the award and is buried in Blankenberge Town Cemetery (A 5). Roland and George are to date the only brothers both to be awarded the Victoria Cross.

Chapter Four

The Advance from Eaucourt l'Abbaye to the capture of Le Sars on 8 October

Le Sars has the dubious distinction of being the nearest village to Bapaume taken by the British in the course of the Somme offensive in 1916. The village, like so many others on the battlefields, was ultimately destroyed in its entirety – one of the few survivors is the remnant of a German regimental memorial in a long ago removed cemetery in a farm yard at the west end of the village.

On 7 October 1916 the 23rd Division, in front of Le Sars, and the 47th (London) Division to its right were the first to make the final advance of 500 yards that resulted in the capture of the village. The British advanced beyond it, but were then held there; despite repeated assaults, the Germans maintained their new positions. The infamous Butte de Warlencourt, situated some 650 yards from Le Sars Communal Cemetery, at the eastern end of the village, dominated the battlefield.

Le Sars in 1919. (*Author's collection*)

The introduction of the 23rd Division to the Somme battle

The 23rd Division was formed in 1914 and along with 21st, 22nd, 24th, 25th and 26th Divisions formed Kitchener's Third New Army (K3): unlike K1 and K2, these formations were not given territorial sub titles as, for example, the 15th (Scottish) and the 16th (Irish), etc. The infantry was provided by battalions of north country and midland county regiments, organised to form 68, 69 and 70 brigades. After many months of training, on 23 August 1915 the Division commenced embarkation for France. Their war was about to commence seriously.

The Division completed its arrival in France in early September 1915 and immediately took up line holding operations near Armentières. It stayed up in French Flanders and before moving south held a line just north of Vimy Ridge. From there it arrived in Vaux (on the

The area of fighting covered by this section. Le Sars is in the centre, the quarry (la Carrière) upper left, the site of Destremont Farm (Ferme du Château) centre bottom left and the frequently mentioned road from Le Sars to Eaucourt l'Abbaye (l'Abbaye d'Eaucourt) can be clearly seen. The Butte de Warlencourt is upper centre right.

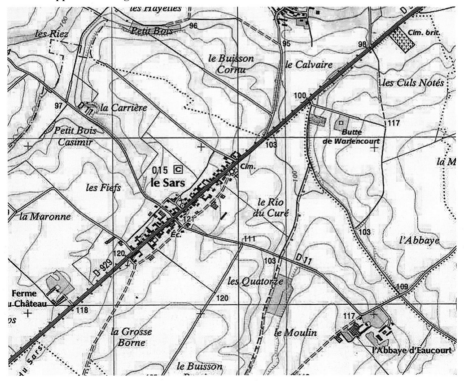

Somme) in late June 1916, where it joined III Corps of Fourth Army. The GOC was Lieutenant General James Melville Babington CB CMG. He was commissioned in the 16th Lancers in 1873 and served in the Bechuanaland Expedition of 1884–85 and in the South African War. Babington was mentioned in despatches for both these campaigns. After the South African War, he was appointed to the New Zealand Defence Force, which he commanded from 1902 until 1907, when he went on retired pay. He returned to the army at the outbreak of war and commanded the 23rd Division for almost its entirety, a relatively unusual feat, especially give as he was quite old, sixty at the outbreak of the war.

Major General JM Babington KCB KCMG was 'dug out' from retirement to be given the command of the 23rd Division. Professor Peter Simkins has commented that Babington was an officer with varied experience and a creditable record, who had spent some time in command of the New Zealand Defence Force (1902–07). Although relatively old, at 61, when appointed GOC of the 23rd Division, he was one of the most successful of Kitchener's selections.

Before the Battle of Flers-Courcelette opened on 15 September 1916, from right to left, the 47th (London), 50th (Northumbrian) and 15th (Scottish) Divisions of III Corps occupied the front line from the southern edge of High Wood to opposite Martinpuich. Two days later, on 17 September, the 23rd Division received orders to hold the line that had been fixed as the left sector of the front held by III Corps. This entailed the relief of the 15th (Scottish) Division and a small part of the line held by the 50th (Northumbrian) Division.

A telling, if somewhat ironic, comment about the difficulties of the relief appear in the 23rd Division's excellent history: ... *as is so often the case after an attack, the exact position of the enemy and our own troops was somewhat obscure.* These Corps sectors had a frontage of some 2000 yards. The reliefs took place on 18 and 19 September, with 69 Brigade taking over the line, 68 Brigade in support and 70 Brigade in reserve. On 19 September the 50th (Northumbrian) Division was on its right and the 1st Canadian Division (Canadian Corps, Reserve Army), who held Courcelette, on the other side of the main Albert-Bapaume Road, was on its left.

The 23rd Division: The taking of Destremont Farm

The occupation of nearby Destremont Farm was deemed an essential preliminary to a successful attack on the small village of Le Sars. The farm was situated on the main Albert-Bapaume road, some 500 yards from the western entrance to Le Sars and a little north of the Bapaume Road.

After an unsuccessful attempt by 70 Brigade to secure the farm on 28 September, a company of the 8th York and Lancasters (8/Y&L), part of the Brigade, was ordered to attack and capture it the following day. The assaulting company assembled on a line some 700–800 yards from its objective. At 5.30 am on the 29th, advancing in two waves at fifty yards apart, the men closed up to the artillery barrage that covered their advance. Moving steadily forward, the attacking lines were within fifty yards of the enemy's position when the artillery lifted to clear the way for the assault. Immediately the German garrison opened fire but the battalion charged the position, killing a large number of the enemy and drove the remainder out of their trenches in considerable disarray. A machine gun, a thousand bombs, a large number of rifles and rounds of ammunition were captured. Subsequently an important engineer dump was discovered near the farm; whilst in the course of the day the success was further augmented when contact was made with the Canadians on their left; the Army boundary was very close to the western edge of the Farm.

Ferme du Château on the south western outskirts of Le Sars – the site of the wartime Destremont Farm. (*Author*)

As was by now customary in these situations, a form of standard operating procedure, the Germans laid down a heavy bombardment on the Farm once it became clear it had been captured, which made the organisation of the defence very difficult. To avoid unnecessary casualties, three platoons were pulled back, leaving a single platoon to defend the position, assisted by two machine guns. The battalion and a section of the 70th Machine Gun Company continued to hold the Farm, all the time under persistent German shelling, until it was relieved by the 10th Duke of Wellington's (10/Dukes) of 69 Brigade on 2 October. The whole operation was a fine example of initiative and determination.

23rd Division: Trenches Flers 1 (Flers Trench) and Flers 2 (Flers Support).
With Destremont Farm in British hands, the next obstacle in front of the troops and between the farm and Le Sars were two major trenches, Flers 1 and Flers 2. An attack on these trenches by 70 Brigade was planned for 1 October, part of a bigger operation that involved XV Corps on the right and the Canadian Corps on the left. The 11th Sherwood Foresters (Nottinghamshire & Derbyshire) (11/Sherwoods) and the 8th King's Own Yorkshire Light Infantry (8/KOYLI) of the Brigade were to attack.

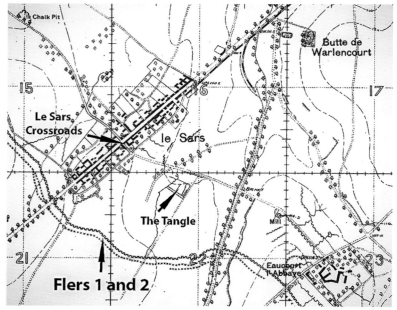

The trenches around Le Sars. (*Author*)

It had been hoped, if no great resistance was encountered in taking the two trenches, that it might be possible to press on and take Le Sars itself. The attack was moderately successful; by the morning of 2 October Flers 1 had been captured and consolidated but Flers 2 was only held south of the Bapaume road. The gains came at a heavy price; the Brigade had taken some 800 casualties and was relieved by 69 Brigade during the night of the 2nd.

The weather now turned bad, with persistent and seemingly unending rain a feature of the remaining weeks of the Somme Offensive. Obviously it had a dispiriting effect on the men but, perhaps more significantly, it turned what passed for trenches into slimy, sticky pits, and what remained of the roads and tracks into treacherous approaches that were hardly any better than the shell torn landscape all around them. Mud, mixed with chalk to form what the BEF regarded as a unique 'Somme mud', was to become the second enemy of the troops of both sides.

For it was not just the men of the BEF and the French army that endured the consequences of the weather conditions. The commander of 1st Battalion Bavarian Reserve Infantry Regiment 16 noted in early October in his regular report that his troops were being severely affected by the extraordinary weather conditions. However, he stated that morale was generally acceptable when all was taken into account. Numerous factors were having a negative effect on morale, such as cold and irregular rations, infrequent reliefs, the effect on the men's nerves of the violence of the British artillery fire, whilst they were suffering from the dispiriting fact that for days their own artillery had been landing shells on their positions. The large number of casualties that were inflicted, the unburied corpses over which they had to pass or even step on and the lack of time out of the line to rest and recuperate all served to sap the spirits of even the best of soldiers. Nevertheless, he felt that his men could still fight and fight well.

The poor conditions did not stop further planning for the 23rd Division to capture Le Sars. This would be a large-scale attack in cooperation with the 47th Division, which would have the nearby Butte de Warlencourt as an objective. The Butte was a chalk mound some sixty feet high, on the slope of the spurs overlooking the Bapaume Road where the Gird Line trenches crossed it. The Butte afforded dominating views of the low ground to the south west and to the rear, towards Bapaume. Its importance was readily appreciated by all the combatants who saw it. Charles Carrington commented:

'... the Butte of Warlencourt terrified us. A dome of gleaming white chalk from which all the vegetation had been blown away

The Butte de Warlencourt in 1917.

by shell fire, it was the most conspicuous object in the landscape by daylight or moonlight. The Butte seemed to tower over you and threaten you. We did three tours in this sector in November and December [1916], the worst in my experience.'

The ghastly weather had transformed the ground into an almost impassable condition, however, such as to render operations on such a large scale impossible. The attack was postponed until 7 October, with the general bombardment starting on 6 October at 3.15 pm.

The northern end of the village of Le Sars viewed from the top of the Butte de Warlencourt. In the distance is Martinpuich and High Wood, both captured in mid September 1916. (*Author*)

In November 1916, Lieutenant Henry Kelly of the 10/Duke of Wellingtons was awarded the Victoria Cross. In the official citation for the award no date appears; but it is believed it was in the action of 3/4 October that he performed the deeds that resulted in his award of this most prestigious of gallantry medals. His citations states:

Lieutenant Henry Kelly VC.
(*www.vconline.org.uk*)

'For most conspicuous bravery in attack. He twice rallied his company under the heaviest fire and finally led the only three available men into the enemy trench and there remained bombing until two of them became casualties and enemy reinforcements had arrived. He then carried his Company Sergeant Major, who had been wounded, back to our trenches, a distance of seventy yards, and subsequently three other soldiers. He set a fine example of gallantry and endurance.'

The V.C. was presented by King George V at Buckingham Palace on 14 February 1917.

Henry Kelly was born in Manchester on 17 July 1887. His parents married in 1887 and Henry was one of eleven children and attended school and college in Manchester. When his father died in 1904, Henry was the sole provider for the family. Henry served in the East Lancashire Engineers (Territorial Force) and was time-expired when he re-enlisted on 5 September 1914. He was commissioned on 12 May 1915 and arrived on the Western Front in France in May 1916. He went on to win an MC and Bar when the Division was serving in Italy towards the end of the war.

His post war career was far from tranquil; he served in the Irish Free State Army on the staff during the Civil War, he qualified as a chartered surveyor, started a grocery chain but went bankrupt in 1931, in due course served as a senior officer in the International Brigade during the Spanish Civil War and served in the army in the UK during the Second World War. He then worked as a valuer, auctioneer and estate agent before retiring to his home area of Manchester; he died in 1960.

Before the main operation could be carried out it was necessary to improve the start line. Two small operations were planned to capture the sections of Flers 1 and 2 still held by the enemy; earlier the Germans had been able to make a foothold in a short length of Flers 1 to the south of the Bapaume road. These operations by 69 Brigade, carried out in the evening of 3 October, failed – and at a heavy cost. The 10 /Dukes suffered twenty-eight killed and 111 others wounded or missing and the 8th Yorkshire Regiment (8/Yorks) had sixty casualties. The Division's casualties for the relatively small-scale actions of 1 to 3 October came to some 1,000 men.

On the afternoon of 3 October the 23rd Division took over the front held by the 50th Division; 149 Brigade was relieved by 68 Brigade. The Division now held Flers 1 for a hundred yards south of the Bapaume Road and 400 yards to the north of it. Beyond that, and to the right, the Division held around 1000 yards of Flers 2. These lines were to be the jumping off points for their forthcoming attack on Le Sars.

From 4 October the weather improved, there being little rain and high winds. Two days later, on 6 October, the day before the main attack to capture the village, the web of trenches called The Tangle, on the eastern side of Le Sars, were occupied by a company of the 11/NF, 68 Brigade. The company came under heavy fire and had to be withdrawn; nevertheless, The Tangle fell the next day, a tank playing a prominent role in its capture.

The attack of 7 October on Le Sars and the Butte de Warlencourt
For Phase One of the attack on 7 October, III Corps' 47th and 23rd Divisions had first to make an advance of about five hundred yards, which would involve the capture of about half of Le Sars. The remainder of the village was to be secured when the attack was resumed against the Butte de Warlencourt and the Gird trenches as far west as the junction of the Gird and Flers trench systems. Zero hour was set for 1.45 pm on 7 October. When the preliminary bombardment started on 6 October it became evident that the Germans had brought more guns into action, judging by the increase in volume of their persistent shelling. III Corps' attack of 7 October was on a three divisional front. On the right of the 47th Division was the 41st Division of XV Corps, who were to attack northerly, in the direction of Luisenhof Farm.

The 47th (1/2nd London) Division
Whilst the 23rd Division had taken Destremont Farm and was now in a position to attack Le Sars, on its right the 47th Division had completed its occupation of Flers Support Trench on 4 October and, after dark on

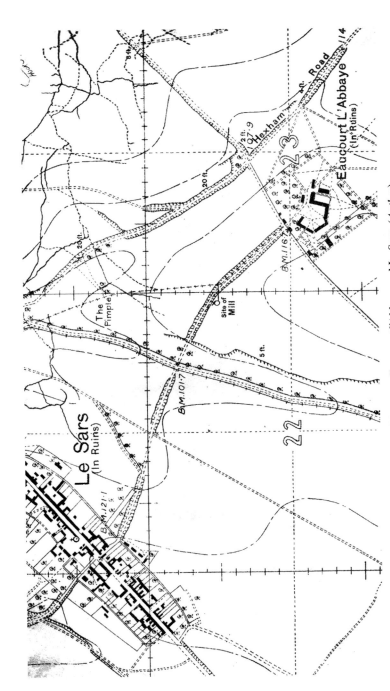

The 'Site of the Mill', centre of the map – on the road between Eaucourt l'Abbaye and Le Sars. (*Author*)

the 5th, had pushed forward its line to include the ruined mill north-west of Eaucourt l'Abbaye. This mill was some 800 yards east of Le Sars, situated next to the Eaucourt l'Abbaye-Le Sars road.

The main German line of defence opposite the Division was the Gird Line, running north-west from Gueudecourt to Warlencourt and which included the Butte de Warlencourt. Anticipating an attack on this important position, the Germans had dug a new trench across their front over the high ground north of Eaucourt l'Abbaye and extending westward into the valley. Named Diagonal Trench, this was to be the first objective of 140 Brigade; their final objective was the Gird Line, including the Butte itself, situated some 660 yards from Le Sars. The centre of this objective lay about 500 yards to the east, half way between the British line and the Butte. The 8th London Regiment (Post Office Rifles) – (8/Londons) – was to secure Diagonal Trench, the 15th London Regiment (PWO Civil Service Rifles), (15/Londons) and 7th London Regiment, (7/Londons) (in order from the right), were then to push

The battlefield from the Butte de Warlencourt to Eaucourt l'Abbaye. Eaucourt l'Abbaye is centre left, the mill was located approximately behind the water sprinkler in the field. Between the Butte and Eaucourt is the site of Butte Trench, The Tail and Snag Trench, with The Pimple being located to the left of the trees running top to bottom in the centre. It was across this ground the Londoners had to attack. (*Author*)

on for the final objective, with the 6th London Regiment (6/Londons) in support.

The attack started as planned at 1.45 pm on 7 October 1916. The whole attacking line came under very heavy fire from Diagonal Trench, some at least of the garrison of which were likely armed with automatic rifles. On the left, the companies of the 8/Londons, followed by the 7/Londons, tried to advance down the slope, forward of the mill, but met, in addition to fire from Diagonal Trench, the full force of enemy artillery and machine-gun fire. This was cleverly sited in depth so as to bring a withering crossfire to bear over the ground and slopes leading up to the Butte. The enemy had magnificent observation over the ground of the advance and made full use of it.

In spite of the intensive fire from the Germans, not a man turned back and some got right up under the Butte; but these were not seen again. The only permanent gain, on the left, were a few posts pushed out from the mill. These were established as strong points in order to keep in contact with the 23rd Division, who advanced along the line of the main road and succeeded in capturing the ruins of Le Sars. On the right some progress was made and a line was established along the sunken road leading north-east from Eaucourt l'Abbaye to La Barque, where a mixed force of the 15/Londons and 8/Londons was organised, commanded by Captain GG Bates of the 15/Londons. A few posts were established near the La Barque Road, in touch with the 41st Division. In summary, the attack of the 47th Division had succeeded on its right but on the left, where they faced the formidable Butte de Warlencourt, it had failed.

The Division's 140 Brigade had suffered very severely in this operation. The following day it was relieved of the left portion of their line by 142 Brigade. However, it was found to be impossible to relieve the 6/Londons' detachment in the advanced posts, and so it was left in its unenviable position until 142 Brigade attacked past them. The 47th Division was due to be relieved by the 9th (Scottish) Division; but first it was hoped to improve the position on the divisional left before the relief took place. The 142 Brigade, therefore, was to make another attempt on 8 October to seize Diagonal Trench and, if successful, were to assault the Butte itself. Only in this, their last operation in this third phase of the Battle of the Somme, did battalions of 142 Brigade attack under the control of their own brigade commander, Brigadier General Lewis.

On 8 October at 9.00 pm, after one minute's intense bombardment, the 21st London Regiment (First Surrey Rifles) (21/Londons) and the 22nd London Regiment (The Queen's) (22/Londons), made the attack. The 21/Londons advanced to within 200 yards of Diagonal Trench without a casualty, then, all at once, the full force of the German

The Butte de Warlencourt today. (*Author*)

machine guns was turned on them, with devastating effect. It seemed that the short bombardment had alerted the enemy to the forthcoming attack. On the left, three companies of the 22/Londons entered Diagonal Trench without great opposition; however, their hold on the position was untenable and success was ultimately limited to the establishment of several strong points some hundred yards short of the objective.

The objectives had not been secured; and the Division's fighting in the Somme 1916 was now over. The 47th Division was relieved and thus the Butte was not to be captured by them despite their heroics. The Division was the last to fight in High Wood and the first to face the dominant 'hillock' of the Butte de Warlencourt. This feature was not captured during the Battle of the Somme, despite being attacked successively by three other divisions. It was only when the Germans made a voluntary withdrawal to the Hindenburg Line at the end of February 1917 that it was occupied – and was made quite insignificant by the fact that the Germans fell back to a new line twenty-five or so kilometres to the east of it. The defenders of the Butte foiled attacks by four divisions of the British Army in the autumn of 1916; the Butte remained German.

The 23rd Division
This Division achieved the striking success of 7 October. Its task was the capture of the village of Le Sars. In conjunction with the Canadians on the left, it was also planned to secure the Flers 1 and Flers 2 trench systems. The Canadians were not to attack until the following day, ie

8 October, and this subsidiary attack would not be carried out until Le Sars had been captured on the previous day.

As a visitor will observe, Le Sars then and now was strung out on either side of the Albert-Bapaume Road; the divisional attack was to be from the left and from the right. The left part of the Division's attack ran in the direction of the road through the village; the right would be on a north east heading and included the east end of Le Sars, with the 47th Division's attack on their right. In front of the right advance, however, were two major obstacles – the previously mentioned Tangle trenches, almost due east of the centre of the village, and a sunken road leading to Le Sars from the south east, just in front of these trenches, which was the road from Eaucourt l'Abbaye to Le Sars. Enfilade fire from the southern side of the village was anticipated.

The Division's attack was to be made by 68 Brigade on the right and 69 Brigade on the left. The battle headquarters for each brigade were established in Martinpuich, captured at the opening of the 15 September offensive, with each brigade deploying two battalions in the line, the remaining battalions held in support and reserve. The attack would not be simultaneous along the whole front. In each brigade, the right battalion would advance first, the attack being in two phases.

On the right, the 12/DLI of 68 Brigade were to advance and capture the Tangle and the sunken road east of Le Sars. Simultaneously, on the left, an attack by the 9/Yorks of 69 Brigade would secure the village south of the central crossroads. If all went to plan, the 13/DLI would push forward between the leading battalions to capture the north of the village; whilst the 11/West Yorks, advancing at zero plus twenty minutes, would capture Flers 2, the Flers Support Trench, north of the main road.

The attack was to be supported by the artillery of the 23rd and 50th Divisions in conjunction with that of the 47th on the right. The barrage would be opening on a line 400 yards in advance of the infantry and move forward at a general rate of fifty yards per minute. Special barrages were arranged to assist the 9/Yorks in the initial stages. A tank was also assigned to assist 68 Brigade.

At zero hour, 1.45 pm, 68 Brigade, on the right, sent forward the 12/DLI in four waves, supported by its tank, which reached the British front line a minute after the infantry had advanced. The tank did excellent service in assisting in the clearance of The Tangle; but, after turning left at the sunken Eaucourt l'Abbaye – Le Sars road beyond, it was hit by a shell and destroyed. Enfilade fire from the area of the road was substantial, the advance was checked, but at least The Tangle had been captured.

For Fourth Army's operations on 7 October, only one tank was deployed, the one allocated to the 23rd Division in capturing The Tangle. It was D2 (Serial Number 539) and was commanded by Lieutenant HR Bell.

The tank and its commander had been involved in the first use of tanks on 15 September, but then the tank had ditched before it reached its starting point near Delville Wood. Bell was injured and the tank damaged. Nevertheless, thirty-seven days later both he and it were successfully back in action.

The tank was driven on the road from Martinpuich to a point some 900 yards short of Eaucourt l'Abbaye, where it branched left and was steered to a point halfway along the sunken road from Eaucourt l'Abbaye to Le Sars. The Tangle was just short of this road and was Bell's first objective. He successfully assisted in clearing The Tangle but then, when turning his attention to the action in Le Sars, the tank was hit by a shell. Three members of the crew were wounded but Bell escaped unhurt, whilst the tank caught fire and was destroyed. The Official History noted the tank's value and Bell's control of it in helping to achieve the capture of Le Sars.

The site of The Tangle is in the foreground, to the south east of Le Sars. The L'Abbaye d'Eaucourt to Le Sars road is on the right, leading to the crossroads in the village. (*Author*)

On the left, the 9/Yorks, advancing behind the barrage, entered and initially stormed into the southern end of the village. The enemy were surprised and were subject to an onslaught of bombs and bayonets. However, before the attack reached the cross roads German resistance stiffened and the rate of advance was slowed. The fighting had been in progress for half an hour or so; the fact that the 9/Yorks had been held up was passed down the chain of command and one of the companies of the 13/DLI were ordered to attack the crossroads in the village from the south. Heavy machine-gun fire met this attack; but persistence saw the 13/DLI reach the crossroads at about 2.30 pm, about the same time as the 9/Yorks, who had successfully fought their way through the village. The enemy's position had been weakened, so that the 12/DLI were able to rush forward and occupy the Le Sars to Eaucourt l'Abbaye road.

To the north of the road, as planned, at zero plus twenty the 11/West Yorks attacked Flers Support/Flers 2. Two companies were in the first wave, attacking from Flers 1; the remaining two companies were in support, advancing from Destremont Farm. The attack was subject to overwhelming machine-gun and artillery fire. Of the two companies attacking from Destremont Farm, only two unwounded officers and thirty men reached Flers 1. The attack had failed, apart from taking some communication trenches that lead to Flers 2.

The 10/Duke of Wellingtons arrived to reinforce the Yorkshire battalions and were to play a part in the later stages of the fighting on this flank. With the 9/Yorks under Major Barnes having secured their position in the southern half of the village, they were also able to assist the attack on Flers 2. A combined attack was hastily put together. This third attack on the left met with instant success. The German defence broke. The demoralised Germans abandoned Flers 2, either hiding or streaming across the open ground, where many of them were mown down by rifles, machine guns or shells. Few survived, with some seventy or eighty being shot from a machine gun positioned at the Le Sars crossroads; 69 Brigade had taken its objectives and it now turned to consolidating its gains.

On the right of the attack, 68 Brigade met little resistance. Captain Clark of the 13/DLI, after leaving a platoon in the sunken road, moved through the whole village with the remainder of the two companies at little cost. To protect the rear of the advance from Germans who had hidden away in the numerous dugouts and reinforced cellars, bombs were dropped down them. The eastern limits of the village were reached without difficulty. At 3.40 pm, when it was reported that no sign of the enemy could be seen, patrols were sent to vantage points that gave views of the Butte de Warlencourt and the surrounding countryside.

A view from the south east of the sunken road leading into the crossroads at Le Sars, scene of horrendous fighting on 7 October 1916. (*Author*)

Work immediately began to establish a set of posts to guard the village from counter attack both from the east and north east. By 7.50 pm it was reported that these posts were in place but that contact had not been made with the posts established by 69 Brigade to secure the north western flank of the village. A company of the 11/Northumberland Fusiliers, supported by two machine guns, filled the gap.

At this point Lieutenant Colonel ME Lindsey, CO of the 13/DLI, asked Brigade for two fresh companies and a tank in order to attack the Butte from the west; these reinforcements were not available, Le Sars, however, was now firmly held but, as we have seen, the attack by the 47th Division had failed. The Butte was still in German hands.

The night of the 7th was spent developing the defences of the newly captured ground in preparation for the continuation of the operation the next day. Much of this work was carried out by the sterling efforts of two companies of the 8th Seaforth Highlanders (8/Seaforths) and two companies of the 9th South Staffordshire (9/South Staffs).

69 Brigade's task in the early hours of 8 October was to capture the rest of the Flers 1 and 2 trenches still occupied by the Germans on the left flank of the 23rd Division; and to effect a junction with the Canadians on their left, who were attacking at the same time. A quarry on the Pys road, situated in front of this junction was to be seized. At 4.50 am the Brigade attacked, along with the Canadians. A and D companies of the 8/York & Lancs, attached to 69 Brigade, who had taken over the line during the night, commenced to bomb up the two trenches, with

The quarry on the north western outskirts of Le Sars. (*Author*)

immediate success, as far as the Army boundary. A post was established that commanded the quarry on the Pys road, 750 yards north west of Le Sars. Fifty prisoners were taken, along with three machine guns, and contact was established with the Canadians. The quarry was free of enemy but it was decided not to occupy it, as any troops there would be exposed to enemy fire.

The 23rd Division had now completed the capture of all the objectives that had been assigned to it. In the actions of 7 and 8 October, eleven officers, 517 other ranks and eight machine guns were captured; nearly all the prisoners came from the 360th, 361st and 362nd Regiments of the 4th Ersatz Division. The 23rd Division reported 627 casualties of all ranks, of which 428 – approximately two thirds of the total – came from 69 Brigade, reflecting the fierce fighting in Le Sars itself.

Congratulatory messages poured into divisional headquarters. These included one from the Fourth Army commander, General Rawlinson: *Please convey to all ranks of the 23rd Division my congratulations and best thanks for their fine performance yesterday.* The GOC of the 15th Division wrote to offer *hearty congratulations on your success* and the 50th Division's GOC added his praise: *congratulations from all ranks of the 50th Division on your excellent fight and subsequent capture of Le Sars.* Amongst all these laudatory messages arrived one that showed that the mundane administration of war had to be carried on, whether a major action was underway or not. An urgent message was received in the middle of the fighting for possession of Le Sars. *Your return of tents etc. on charge due at 12 noon today not yet received. Expedite. Urgent.*

Mission accomplished, the 23rd Division left the Somme front, its future lying in the relative calm of the Ypres Salient. On 9 October it was relieved by the 15th (Scottish) Division.

The 47th (London) Division

On that same day, the South African Brigade of the 9th (Scottish) Division relieved 140 and 142 Brigades of the 47th Division. The South African Brigade had been largely rebuilt after the huge losses that it had suffered in Delville Wood in the middle days of July; now it was to have to absorb even more casualties in attacks on the Butte.

The 47th (London) Division had finished its part on the Somme at a cost of 296 officers and 7,475 other ranks killed, wounded, or missing. They had played their part in the successful advance of III Corps, moving the line forward nearly three miles, and capturing, on the way, two German defence systems of prime importance. The division's artillery remained in action for a few days longer – this was quite usual when a division was relieved – and, together with two brigades of the 1st Division's artillery, supported the unsuccessful attack of the 9th Division on the Butte on 12 October. After this they too were relieved and assembled in the Behencourt area, preparing to march northwards.

Every branch of the Division had been taxed to the uttermost during the Somme operations. The lengthy summary in its divisional history of its part in the Somme Offensive provides an insight into the problems that the troops of the BEF encountered, not only from the resolute defence offered by the Germans but, as summer went into autumn and the rains came, the conditions of the roads and the ground became truly horrendous. Its experience was typical of most, if not all, of the formations of all nationalities that fought on the Somme, especially in the latter, autumn, weeks,

Its artillery was continuously in action from the middle of August under often exhausting conditions; guns were crowded forward in positions which offered little or no cover and accommodation and were kept constantly at work firing at difficult targets or providing hastily-prepared barrages for local operations. Difficulty of transport hit the artillery harder than any other branch of the service. As the weather grew worse, the few forward tracks were almost lost in the general morass, and convoys from batteries and divisional ammunition column had to plunge, vehicles up to their axles in mud, over the shell-torn ground that lay between the head of the made-up roads and their gun positions. Providing the stable platform for the guns, essential to their accuracy, was also very difficult. Before they could get back to their open line, they had to take their place in a solid train of traffic that moved slowly along the winding road that led back from Bazentin towards Fricourt.

The Rev. David Railton was a chaplain attached to 141 Brigade (47th Division); he won the MC for bringing in a wounded officer and two other ranks when under enemy fire. Railton was the owner of the famous 'Padre's Flag', the Union Flag that was used at the funerals of many men of the 47th Division in the field, and which was used on Armistice Day 1920 at the funeral of the Unknown Warrior. The flag had been put to many uses by the Division, from serving as the cover of a rough communion table to helping to decorate the stage at concerts behind the line.

It was Railton's inspiration that led to the idea of bringing home from the Western Front an unknown warrior (as the Royal Naval Division served in France, along with the Royal Naval Air Service and, for example, Royal Marines Artillery, it was quite possible that the man chosen could have come from any of the services, hence 'warrior' and not 'soldier') and burying him amongst the great in Westminster Abbey. It would be a symbol of the sacrifice of the servicemen who had given their all for their country; and a place of pilgrimage for the many relatives who never knew where their loved one lay. At the Armistice Day service in 1921 the flag was solemnly dedicated and placed by representatives of the 47th Division above the grave of the Unknown Warrior in Westminster Abbey.

David Railton became Vicar of Margate after the war and served in several other parishes around the country; he retired in 1945 and was killed in a railway accident in 1955, aged 70.

The Unknown Warrior lies in Westminster Abbey on 11 November 1920. Present at the burial were leading politicians, senior military figures and members of the Royal Family, led by King George V. This large painting, which hangs in Committee Room 10 in the Houses of Parliament, is by the artist Frank O Salisbury, who attended the burial and made a sketch of the scene at the time.

Battlefield conditions had changed remarkably since 1915. On 26 September 1915, the night after the Battle of Loos opened, transport could use any road right up to the front line. By contrast, nearly a fortnight passed after 15 September 1916 before a single mule track was available over the crest of the ridge on which High Wood stood. The long distances over which the infantry carrying parties had to struggle every night with supplies of ammunition and food were a heavy strain on the brigade in reserve. At this stage the use of pack animals and limbered wagons for the supply of the forward area was still in its infancy. On several days when the road to Bazentin was drying up after rain the mud became so sticky that the motorcyclist despatch riders stuck in it and the despatches had to be carried by mounted orderlies. The supply of water was a matter of the greatest difficulty, as the line advanced and the stock of petrol cans was exhausted. Forward of Bazentin le Grand Wood, where large tanks were filled from time to time by water lorries that had to take their turn in the seemingly endless stream of traffic, every drop of water had to be man-handled forward from there. Weary carrying parties struggled through the slime with two petrol cans full of water, weighing something over 40 lbs, and returned exhausted, often only to be sent back with another load.

The field ambulances worked under conditions of the utmost difficulty owing to the impossibility, during the greater part of the battle, of using wheeled transport further forward than the main dressing station at Bottom Wood. During the first phase wounded had to be carried by stretcher bearers from the dressing station at High Alley to that at Flat Iron Copse, and often as far as Bottom Wood, a journey sometimes taking five or six hours. The absence of landmarks and the difficulty of locating regimental aid-posts established by the battalion medical officers during the advance added to the bearers' troubles. However, things could improve; at least for the attack that began on 1 October The Cough Drop, now accessible by day and providing excellent shelter, was selected as the advanced dressing station. There was a wonderful German dugout built there, with three entrances in the side of a bank that provided accommodation for some seventy stretcher cases.

On 10 October the brigades were billeted in Albert, Franvillers and Lavieville. Here they were inspected by their Corps commander, Lieutenant General Pulteney. Four days later they left Albert for a journey northward. On the same day the Divisional Artillery, now relieved in the line, assembled around Behencourt-Frechencourt, preparatory to marching to join the Division in Second Army's area. In a farewell message, General Sir Henry Rawlinson wrote:

'The operations carried out by the 47th Division during the Battle of the Somme have been of material assistance to the Fourth Army, and I desire to congratulate all ranks on their gallantry and endurance. The capture of High Wood and the trenches beyond it on September 15th and 16th was a feat of arms deserving of high praise, whilst the attack and capture of Eaucourt l'Abbaye on 1st, 2nd and 3rd October, involving as it did very hard fighting, was a success of which the division may be justly proud. The Divisional Artillery has rendered excellent service in supporting the infantry attacks and in establishing the barrages on which success so often depends.

I regret that the Division have now left the Fourth Army, but at some future time I trust it may be my good fortune to again have them under my command to add to the successes they have won at Loos, at High Wood, and at Eaucourt l'Abbaye.'

In the course of the first week of October the line had progressed from Eaucourt l'Abbaye to Le Sars, including the capture of Destremont Farm. Since the capture of Martinpuich on 15 September, the front line had moved forward approximately two miles over a period of some three weeks. But still standing ominously in front of the attacking troops lay the formidable Butte de Warlencourt, which had already successfully frustrated attempts to capture it.

As for the Germans, the recent daily returns had seen a notable increase in reports that the condition of the troops was declining. Over and above

Life begins to return to a form of 'normal' in Le Sars after the war. (*Author*)

LE SARS (P.-de-C) — Baraquement Carpentier, épicerie, tabac

battle casualties, the number of sick, the number of cases of diarrhoea and the general state of morale meant that the commander of the 1st Bavarian Battalion felt he should express his concerns about the welfare of the men and the impact that the conditions were having on their battle worthiness. The regimental commander could do no more than pass this further up the line and prepare his ever-decreasing number of troops ready for future attacks. These exhausted troops successfully beat back further attacks before they were eventually relieved, a tribute to the quality of the German soldier. But the situation was worrying, for the balance of the war had clearly become one of materiel – of machines – against man

Perhaps the final comments on the capture of Le Sars should come from Brigadier General Lambert, then GOC 69 Brigade. In his 'Report on Operations of 69th Brigade at the capture of Le Sars on 7th and 8th October 1916', he strongly disagreed with the account in *The Times,* which reported that the operation to capture Le Sars was effected without difficulty, the enemy freely surrendering. Lambert concluded that this impression was wrong and that the enemy surrendered only when compelled to do so and after offering as much resistance as they were able. An invitation to *The Times* correspondents was extended to spend time in the future with the troops in front of brigade headquarters so that they could experience what really happens in the field of conflict. One wonders if this offer was ever taken up.

The ruins of Le Sars after its capture by British troops.

Chapter Five

The further attempts to capture the Butte de Warlencourt: October and November 1916

'But the BUTTE-DE-WARLENCOURT had become an obsession. Everybody wanted it. It loomed large in the minds of the soldiers in the forward area and they attributed many of their misfortunes to it. The newspaper correspondents talked about "that Miniature Gibraltar". So it had to be taken.'

Roland Boys Bradford

The attack of 7 October: 47th (London) Division
The 7 October saw the village of Le Sars taken from the Germans as a result of the sterling efforts of the 23rd Division attacking into the village, principally advancing up the Post Road, the road between Albert to Bapaume; theirs was the left of III Corps' attack. To the

Aerial picture of the Butte de Warlencourt, dated 16 October 1916.

23rd's Division's right was the 47th (London) Division, which faced the main German line of defence, here called the Gird Line, running north-west from Gueudecourt to Warlencourt, and which included the Butte de Warlencourt. This unsuccessful attack was covered in the previous chapter, on the attacks of 7 October on Le Sars and the Butte: it was to be the first of several aiming to capture the early medieval man-made mound. Two days after the attack failed the 47th Division left the Somme battlefields with 140 and 142 Brigades replaced in the line by the South African Brigade. The 47th was the first of a total of four divisions that were to attack over the ground leading to the Butte. The South Africans' time in the line here was going to prove to be equally as terrifying as that of the 47th Division, ending a mere ten days later, when they also were withdrawn from the line, to nearby High Wood, much damaged by their experience.

The arrival of the South Africans. The attack of 12 October 1916
The personnel might have changed but the aim of Fourth Army had not; the attacks would continue. At 10.00 pm on 8 October Fourth Army issued orders for an attack along its line in order to secure all the remaining objectives of 7 October, to take place on 12 October. In the intervening time III Corps took the opportunity of relieving the 47th and 23rd Divisions with the 9th (Scottish) and the 15th (Scottish) divisions, which meant that the newly arrived 9th (Scottish) Division had very little time in which to prepare for the next attack. An appeal was made by its GOC for a postponement of forty-eight hours; but his appeal fell on deaf ears. The Royal Flying Corps tried to assist by carrying out as much photographic work as possible in order to locate new German trenches and positions; but it was now autumn on the Somme and, as anyone who has visited the area in the autumn will appreciate, the light at that time is often poor and the task was very difficult. Such aerial work was made perilous by the increasing capability of German air power in the skies above the Somme. Until about mid-September the RFC and French air force had dominated the skies over the battlefield but now things were changing in favour of the Germans.

More than two months had elapsed since the 9th Division had fought at nearby Longueval, notably in Delville Wood, and in this period continuing attacks had seen the British slowly take German held territory north and east of that village. Behind the British front line, consequently, was the accumulated debris and destruction of three months of horrific fighting, the whole area ravaged by shell fire, covered in the detritus of war, the road to the front line sprinkled with scattered body fragments and with the putrid smell of decomposing bodies filling the air. The line

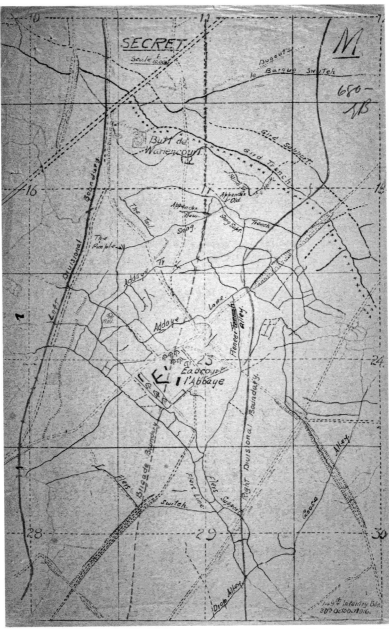

Map of the battlefields from 149 Brigade's records dated 30 October 1916 (*National Archives*)

previously held by the 47th Division was now held by the 9th; 26 Brigade on the right, the South African Brigade on the left, the line situated to the north of Eaucourt l'Abbaye. The divisional boundary on the left was the road to the west of Eaucourt that ran from the Butte de Warlencourt to Martinpuich. The South African Brigade's boundary with 26 Brigade ran through the ruins of Eaucourt l'Abbaye. Two companies of the 2nd South African Regiment held the front line and a further two were in the support trenches of the old Flers lines, running along the south west side of Eaucourt l'Abbaye.

New orders were received on 9 October. The 9th Division's main objective was the capture of the Butte de Warlencourt, including Snag and Tail trenches, The Pimple and the trench lying to the far side of the Butte. The Nose ran back from Snag Trench towards the Butte and The Pimple was at the western end of Snag Trench/Pimple Alley.

Zero on 12 October was fixed for 2.05 pm and the attack, which was to be led by the 7/ Seaforths and the 2nd South African Regiment, was to be covered by a creeping barrage. The left flank would be covered by a smoke screen between Le Sars and the Butte, which was to be laid down by the 15th (Scottish) Division. To deceive the Germans a Chinese attack was arranged for 11 October; this artillery attack was in essence a ruse. The same sort of bombardment that would accompany an infantry attack would be fired, moving over the enemy's positions; but then it would suddenly return back to the enemy front line and, hopefully, catch troops who had emerged from cover to man the trenches, anticipating an assault. This Chinese attack worked quite well, resulting in several machine guns showing their positions.

The attack was launched in October drizzle. One minute after zero the 6th Bavarian Reserve Division's supporting artillery replied with a heavy bombardment that cut all the infantry telephone wires and broke all their communications lines. The only reports received came from the artillery or Royal Flying Corps. Only twenty-nine minutes after the attack commenced an artillery observer reported that the attack had failed; by around 8.30 pm that evening it was certain that it had failed.

On the right the 7/Seaforths, whose suffering was made worse by British shells falling short, had a first objective which lay hundreds of yards from the British front line, over ground perfectly suited for machine-gun and rifle fire. They came under sustained machine-gun fire as soon as the attack commenced and, although the 10/Argylls pushed forward to reinforce them, barely two hundred yards of ground were gained. In the evening, those who could straggled back to their own trenches; but a mixed party of the Argylls dug in some 150 yards forward of the original front line and this new line was held and strengthened.

On the left the South Africans met a similar fate. Their 2nd Regiment, followed by their 4th, were checked by long-range machine-gun fire, whilst smoke drifting from the barrage laid on the Butte worked against them, making it difficult to maintain direction. The Germans also adopted the practice of locating their machine guns (or at least a good proportion of them) some distance behind the front line trenches and dealt with the British attack at long distance: the ground over which the attack had to come was perfectly suited for this type of cover by machine guns. People tend to forget that a machine gun is an area weapon with a long range; in many respects, so long as within range, the further back the weapon is the more effective and economical it is.

The momentum of the South African advance dissipated before the first objective could be gained. As the leading battalions of the Brigade were in fact nowhere near reaching the first objective, the 3rd South African Regiment was ordered to relieve them, whilst the 1st Regiment was moved up in support. The relief was extremely difficult due to the congested state of the communication trenches and the lack of reliable

Private EC Babb's 'death penny'. (*Author*)

Private EC Babb 2nd Regiment South African Infantry, died 12 October 1916. (*Author*)

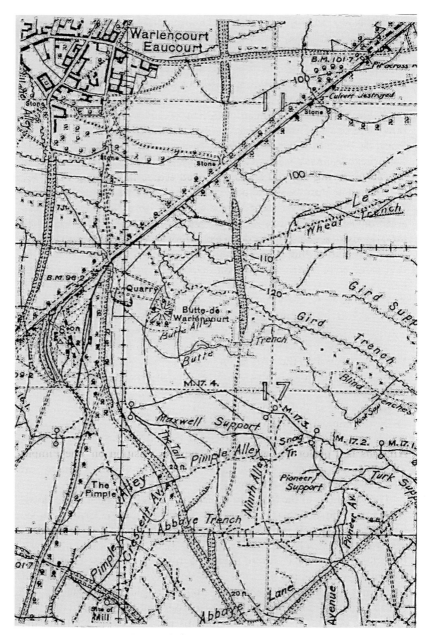

Location of The Pimple and of several of the key trenches involved in the attacks on the Butte. The road from Le Sars to Eaucourt l'Abbaye is bottom left.

guides; it was not until dawn on 13 October that that what remained of the 2nd and 4th Regiments were brought back to the relative safety of High Wood.

The attack on 12 October by the 9th Division had failed; it simply evaporated, the barrage failing to destroy the enemy's trenches and machine-gun positions. The Germans appeared to be well prepared and ready for the attack, undoubtedly warned by the bombardment, and they now appeared to be accustomed and ready for afternoon attacks. The Butte de Warlencourt had survived its second main attack unscathed; but attacks against it were to continue.

The following day the Division issued orders that Strong Point 93, known as The Pimple, was to be reconnoitred with the aim of occupying it. The Pimple was a mound, some sixty feet long, twelve feet wide, and from twelve to fifteen feet high. A patrol reached The Pimple with little opposition and found it deserted, although it showed clear signs of occupation, including gun emplacements and a deep dugout. The 3rd Regiment were instructed the following evening, under the cover of dark, to take possession of The Pimple and link it up with the British line. Accordingly, early on the night of 14 October, a company of the 3rd South African Regiment successfully reached and occupied it. The Germans reacted vigorously; the occupants were heavily bombed by Germans moving along the trenches that connected it to their lines. Soon after dawn on the 15th an enemy party was seen approaching the feature but was quickly dispersed by machine-gun fire. B Company continued to hold The Pimple and the associated captured trenches until it was relieved by A Company on the night of the 15th. The Regiment's casualties came to three officers and thirty-five other ranks. It was a rare bright spot in British offensive activity in this area at the time: the South Africans had performed admirably. The new position on The Pimple gave excellent views right up to the Butte and was a perfect location on which to position machine guns.

The battalions of the BEF had shown great determination – as indeed, it has to be said, had their counterparts in the French and German armies on the Somme at this time. Manpower shortages were a serious problem for everyone as well; the British Official History notes that only a few battalions could muster more than 400 men for an attack (sometimes called 'bayonets' – ie men with rifles actually on the ground). A full strength ('up to establishment') battalion might deploy about 800 bayonets for a full scale battalion assault out of a full strength of 1,000 men, give or take: so, in effect, battalions were attacking with half the manpower that would have been deployed by a battalion on 1 July 1916. In addition, many of the men fighting in these latter stages of the Somme

Offensive were only half-trained reinforcements. Air assistance, amongst other things the important work of identifying new German positions, had been severely restricted by poor visibility. Finally, the nature of trench warfare had changed: although there were trenches, these were far from the formidable structures that the Germans had developed over twenty months or so of occupation and which had faced the British on 1 July. Less comfortable for the occupants – of whom there were far fewer in the forward 'trenches' – and providing all sorts of command, communications and supply problems, what were sometimes nothing much more than connected shell holes actually provided considerable problems for the attackers as identification of lines and targets became increasingly difficult. This looser system of defence required a high standard of military competency and morale, and this the Germans had.

Conscious that most of the early October objectives were still to be captured (obviously including the Butte de Warlencourt), Rawlinson determined to attack again on 18 October. The preliminary bombardment was to start immediately and was to continue up to zero hour. During the night of the 16th the 3rd South African Regiment was relieved from the front line trenches by the 1st. The next assault was timed to commence in the early morning of 18 October, having the same objectives of the 12th.

The attack of the 18 October: 'They had disappeared, none of them ever returned'.

The 18th dawned dull and with rain never far away, like so many mornings on the Somme in autumn. There was no afternoon start time on this occasion. Zero hour was set for 3.40 am, well before sunrise – in short it was a night attack initially but timed to develop in the light of the dawn. Preparations for the assault were once more of a high standard, with forming up positions taped out and compass bearings taken for the direction of the advance – the latter essential, given that it was both at night and in an area short of topographical features except for the Butte itself.

When the attack commenced the moon was obscured by cloud; the men struggled forward into a seemingly impenetrable darkness – except when everything was brightly lit for moments by Very Lights – and frequently fell into the deep, tenuous mud. Rifles and Lewis guns soon become became clogged and as a result bombs and bayonets soon became the main weapons of both assault and defence. In an endeavour to reduce the effectiveness of the German retaliation from the Butte de Warlencourt and to make things difficult for their artillery observers, it and the area around it was covered by smoke and tear gas bombs fired from the front of the neighbouring 15th (Scottish) Division.

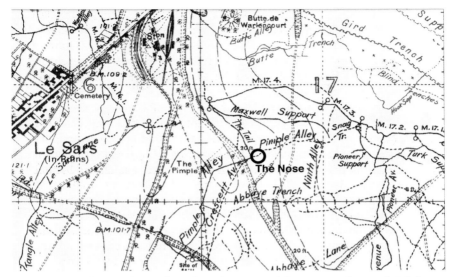

Location of The Tail and Snag Trench, extracted from a trench map dated 1 January 1917. The Nose is indicated by a O.

Present day view over the area of The Tail, Nose and Snag Trench. Note the banking to be climbed to the right of the track. The Butte is at the upper right. (*Author*)

Closer view of the banking to be climbed to reach The Tail, which was located approximately forty metres over the top of the banking. (*Author*)

On the right, finding resistance light, the 5/Camerons, of 26 Brigade, captured Snag Trench to within 200 yards of The Nose, the aptly named junction of Snag Trench and The Nose. In the afternoon a German counter attack from the right secured a footing in the captured trench but they were driven out again after darkness. The prisoners taken belonged to the 104th Regiment of the 40th Division.

To the left of the Camerons was the 1st South African Regiment; the three assaulting companies (from right to left, A, B, and C) of the Regiment were for the most part deployed in No Man's Land. Keeping as close as possible to the barrage, the South Africans advanced, disappearing into the gloom and the rain and for several hours nothing was heard of them. When news did come it told yet again of failure. C Company reached The Nose but were held up by the wire, bombs, and the steep bank in front of the German line. The only surviving officer, himself wounded, saw that there was no hope of success and ordered survivors to pull back to their original front line: its casualties were sixty-nine men out of the hundred who set out.

A and B Companies rapidly moved forward and reached Snag Trench. However, in the darkness and the miserable conditions, they failed to realise that they had reached their objective and, instead of halting and consolidating the gains, continued advancing beyond it and into enemy fire coming from the Butte. They had lost touch with anyone on their flanks, so that in places there were Germans between them and their old front line. With the exception of a few stragglers, all the men of A and B Companies were casualties. A patrol sent out to look for them returned with no information. In a dreadful summary of the South African attack, C Company had failed and with heavy losses and, with the exception of sixteen men getting back to the front line and any who were taken prisoner by the Germans, A and B companies 'had disappeared' according to the South African history or, in the words of the 9th (Scottish) Division's history, with a few exceptions 'none of them ever returned'. The records of the CWGC for those who died in the 1st South African Regiment for the period 18 to 20 October inclusive suggest that about seventy to seventy-five were killed in that date range; of course a number likely died of wounds in the following days and the balance of the casualties would have been prisoners.

At daybreak German machine-gun fire from The Nose saw off an attempt to bomb along the trench leading to the junction of The Nose and Snag Trenches. The area was commanded by the Germans at The Nose and yet this was certainly the key point to any attack. The fight had to continue and the South African mission to take The Nose began again at 5.45 pm. Attacking along Snag Trench and reaching a point twenty-

Towards the close of the action at Ruiter's Kraal on 13 August 1901, Sergeant Major Young, with a handful of men, rushed some kopjes that were being held by Commandant Erasmus and about twenty Boers. On reaching these kopjes the enemy were seen galloping back to another kopje held by the Boers. Sergeant Major Young then galloped on some fifty yards ahead of his party and, closing with the enemy, shot one of them and captured Commandant Erasmus, the latter firing at him three times at point blank range before being taken prisoner.

Lieutenant Alexander Young VC, killed in action on 19th October 1916. (*www.vconline.org.uk*)

He was presented with his medal almost a year later, on 8 August 1902, by the GOC Cape Colony in South Africa. An Irishman (from County Galway), Young enlisted in the Queen's Bays in 1890 and served in India and the Sudan; in due course he became a riding instructor, in Sudan, India and at Shorncliffe, until he received a bad kick from a horse and decided to retire back to Galway. Soon bored, he went out to South Africa, becoming a senior member of the Cape Mounted Police; he won his VC in Basutoland. He retired again, this time farming in Natal; at the outbreak of the war he re-joined once more, was commissioned in the 4th South African Mounted Rifles and took part in Smuts campaign in German South West Africa. Demobilised at the end of that campaign, he then joined the South African Scottish and was despatched, eventually, to France. To say that his career was eventful is surely a major understatement!

Now aged 43, he took part in the early stages of the Battle of the Somme, was wounded and invalided to England. Following his recovery and recuperation in Brighton, he returned to the battle front in September 1916 and was killed in action on 19 October 1916. The VC winner is commemorated on the Thiepval Memorial – the South Africans are the only Dominion whose missing in France are commemorated there, the others having their own such memorials, such as at Neuve Chapelle, Vimy and Villers Bretonneux.

five yards from The Nose, three German machine guns forced the South Africans to return to their original front line. Not to be seen as giving in, a company of the 4th Regiment was despatched in the early hours of the morning of the 19th with instructions to capture The Nose. Snag Trench was occupied; however, a German attack by bombs and flamethrowers at 5.00 am drove the occupants out. Amongst those killed was Lieutenant Alexander Young VC, who won his medal in South Africa in 1901.

At this point, ie the afternoon of 19 October, with but a few exceptions, the South Africans were back in their old front line; the attacks had failed miserably. The Nose had been defended admirably by the Germans and when it was finally occupied over 250 of them were found lying dead in its vicinity. It is evident that German reports about a lack of fighting will at Martinpuich cannot be applied here. The fight that day for Snag Trench was not over, as a further attempt was to be made by a company from the 3rd Regiment. Two machine guns at The Pimple enfiladed Snag Trench, causing panic, and by the afternoon only a few of the enemy were left in that trench. But the Germans and their machine guns still held The Nose.

The position seemed to be impregnable. Yet another failed attack in the afternoon brought to an end the determination to capture The Nose; action to drive the enemy out of the position had failed, amongst other reasons given being an insufficiency of bombs (ie grenades). The situation had become hopeless. the South Africans had run out of men, the mud was so thick and all pervasive that rifles, machine guns and Lewis guns were constantly jamming and the men left on The Pimple had not one working, usable rifle. In many of the trenches the mud was three feet deep and every soldier was utterly exhausted. The South African contribution to the Battle of the Transloy Ridges, 1–18 October, was over. That night the remaining South Africans in the line were relieved and early in the morning of 20 October they were back in High Wood.

The Story of the South African Brigade by John Buchan, which acts as a sort of unofficial history of South Africa's efforts on the Western Front, says that this action was a step too far for the Brigade, poignantly noting, *so ended the tale of the South Africans share in the most dismal of all the chapters of the Somme.* His narrative sums up the situation succinctly. The fighting did not have the swift pace of earlier battles and the men were striving for minor objectives, so that often the action was reduced to isolated struggles, where a handful of men in a mud-filled hole held on until their post was linked up to the front line. Rain, cold, slow reliefs, lack of hot food – indeed lack of any food, had made these episodes a severe test of endurance and devotion. So bad was the mud that each stretcher required eight bearers and runners carrying no heavy equipment and taking up to six hours to cover a thousand yards. The front was never at any one moment clearly defined, leading to a perpetual and inevitable confusion of mind. Buchan concludes that officers led and men followed in a cruel fog of uncertainty. In the ten days from 9 to 19 October, the South African casualties were approximately 1150, including forty-five officers, sixteen of whom were killed. At the end of October the South African Brigade moved north to an area near Arras; but they were to return to the Somme the following February, following the German retreat; and, memorably, once more, during the fraught days of the German spring offensive in March 1918.

During the night of the 19th, which involved in places struggling through communication trenches waist deep in mud, so bad that seriously injured troops could quickly disappear under it, 27 Brigade of the 9th Division took over all the divisional front from 26 Brigade. After an exhausting, sapping struggle to get to the front line, the 6/KOSB were deemed capable of attacking at 4.00 pm the following day, the 20th. Confused fighting followed: The Nose was taken, evacuated and reoccupied. That night the Borderers were firmly established in Snag Trench and a company of the 11/Royal Scots had pushed forward up The Nose, now held for a length of 250 yards. During the evening of that day the task was made much simpler when the Germans withdrew in good order in accordance with the relatively new policy of giving up forward positions of no tactical value rather than fighting on and incurring further losses for no appreciable benefit. The British were really no nearer to capturing the Butte, which stood indomitably behind Snag Trench, the long muddy slopes leading up to it covered in the dead of both sides. The odour of death was everywhere, the sights truly awful. In open ground before Snag Trench a long line of dead men of the London Division was grim evidence of a gallant charge thwarted by machine gun fire.

By the night of 20 October all of the objectives of the attack of the 18th had been secured; the 9th (Scottish) Division still held the line and prepared for yet another attack on the Butte, planned for the 25th. Fortunately, the Division was relieved late on the 24th; it was appreciated that another attack was indeed beyond the capacity of the men. The Division's history concludes:

'The action at the Butte de Warlencourt was the most dismal of operations carried out by the division. In that waste of mud and water, the ground captured though small in extent represented no mean achievement. The Butte remained impregnable, guarded by slime and weather. It may be questionable if the ground gained was worth the cost.'

Sadly, these same views were to be shortly heard again.

Attack of 5 November 1916 – would there be fireworks on the Butte?

By the middle of October, conditions on and behind the battle front were growing ever more ghastly. The ground was so deep in mud that to move one 18-pound gun often required ten or twelve horses. The supplies usually brought by light railway and pack horse, ammunition and more, had to be dragged on sledges improvised of sheets of corrugated iron. The exhausted infantry, at times soaked to the skin for days, all too often had to struggle through the mud under heavy German fire against difficult to find and vaguely defined objectives. Generals Foch, Rawlinson and Gough came to GHQ for a conference on 19 October that discussed the future development of the Somme Offensive. It was decided that, weather permitting, Fourth Army, amongst other objectives, was to secure the Butte de Warlencourt and the Warlencourt Line beyond on 25 October. Not unexpectedly, the weather was to intervene and it was not until 3 November that any temporary improvement in the weather was seen. On 30 October it was decided that the German salient north of Guedecourt and north east of Eaucourt L'Abbaye, together with the Butte de Warlencourt, should be the objectives of an independent operation whenever the weather permitted. First fixed for 2 November, the date was altered to the 5th to coincide with the attacks planned elsewhere on the front by XIV Corps and by the French on their right; although not in the scope of this book, it must not be forgotten that the French army was also heroically fighting. Indeed, if the German army was going to crumble anywhere in these dying days of the Somme Offensive, it would appear to have come closest to that around Sailly-Saillisel and the western side of the huge St Pierre Vaast Wood. Much of the BEF's offensive activity along the Le Transloy Ridge should be seen in the context of the big French push to the British right, seeking to outflank

Another fog over the battlefields. An autumn view from the top of the Butte. (*Author*)

The Butte overlooks the moving of munitions over the shattered battlefield. (*Fonds des albums Valois* – **Pas de Calais**)

Péronne – and thus crucial Somme crossings – from the north. It was not simply as an observer that Foch attended the meeting on the 19th.

The 50th Division went back into the line close to its old stamping ground on 25 October. Relieving the 9th Division, 149 Brigade relieved 26 Brigade on the right, and the 150th relieved 27 Brigade on the left; 151 Brigade was in reserve. The sector taken over by the division lay east and south-east of Le Sars and in the fork formed by the Martinpuich-Warlencourt, Eaucourt and Martinpuich-Le Barque roads. Its left boundary followed the former road and the right the latter, to just north of Eaucourt L'Abbaye, in what was a very irregular front line. The Germans front line was Gird Trench and Gird Support, which ran from north west to south east across the front of the 50th Division and were to the rear of the Butte de Warlencourt.

The Butte was to feature prominently in the Division's activity in November 1916, with its change in appearance in a matter of about two months clearly described by Major EH Veitch in the Division's history.

'...Gird Trench ran east and west from the Albert-Bapaume road towards Gueudecourt. On the left lay the Butte de Warlencourt, a mound or tumulus some forty feet [sic] high, reported to be an ancient burial-place similar to those found on Salisbury Plain. This, in September, when the Battalion first entered the Somme fighting, stood out from the surrounding country as a green, conical-shaped hill. Of little or no strategic importance, except that it provided observation of all the ground towards High Wood, Martinpuich and east of that village, it had been so battered by the daily shelling that all signs of vegetation had now disappeared and it stood a shapeless, pock-marked mass of chalk. Beyond the Gird lay a stretch of undulating country, with Bapaume clearly visible in the distance, and midway, almost hidden in a small valley, was Le Barque. The remainder of the attack frontage held no special feature except for a considerable amount of dead ground to the rear of the objective.'

A heavy gale brought in daybreak on 5 November. As a result of the very poor conditions, when the attack was launched at 9.10 am the infantry had great difficulty in scrambling out of their mud-filled assembly 'trenches', which in some places were thigh deep in the glutinous mess. As 149 and 150 Brigades had been so long in the line, it was the men of 151 Brigade who were to spearhead the assault, using three battalions, supported by two battalions of 149 Brigade, the 4th and 6th Northumberland Fusiliers. The Division's objective was Gird Trench and Gird Support; the three attacking battalions, from right to left, the 8th, 6th and 9th Durham Light Infantry. They were to assemble for the attack in Snag Trench and Snag Support, Maxwell Trench and Tail Trench. The Corps Heavy Artillery concentrated on the Gird Lines, the Butte de Warlencourt and the area between Warlencourt and Le Barque-Thilloy. The objectives of the 6 and 8/DLI were Gird and Gird Support; 9/DLI was given the daunting task of capturing the Butte de Warlencourt and the Quarry just to the west of the Butte. The 4 and 6/NF were to be right and left support battalions, respectively. The remaining battalion of 151 Brigade, the 5/Borders, were in brigade support in Prue and Starfish Trenches.

At zero hour the barrage fell and immediately the troops began to crawl out of their trenches as best as the conditions allowed. The enemy's barrage fell in front of Snag Trench but was not particularly heavy. From both sides of the attack machine-gun fire swept the attackers with great effect; the men found it difficult to advance at anything more than a walking pace through the mud and began to fall at once; whilst cohesion was also extremely difficult as almost each man had to move as his own particular conditions permitted. The 8/DLI, on the right, struggled on but far behind the covering barrage and almost got to the German front line; but its progress was halted by machine-gun fire from both flanks. Finding further advance impossible, they withdrew, under orders, to Snag Trench. Their fight was over, with the German fire being so severe that both wounded and unwounded lay out all day in shell holes or whatever cover they could find, aiming and praying to get back after darkness had fallen. In the centre, the 6/DLI suffered a similar experience except on the left, where some of the battalion entered Gird Trench. On the left the 9/DLI advanced magnificently and carried all their objectives, breaking through two lines of German defences, reaching the Butte and with observers seeing Durham men actually on the Butte. Was this the long hoped for result, going as far back as October? Was the Butte finally to surrender its undefeated tag?

Colonel Bradford, commanding the 9/DLI, recorded their exploits in the 9/DLI War Diary.

'... 9.10am A, B and C Companies crept forward under the artillery barrage and assaulted the enemy's trenches. The assault was entirely successful. By10.30 am we had taken the quarry and had penetrated the Gird Line, our objective. A post was established on the Bapaume road where the left Divisional boundary cut across the Bapaume road, i.e. north west of the Quarry. A machine-gun in a dug-out on the north-eastern side of the Butte held up our advance somewhat, and we attempted many times to bomb this dug-out. Telephonic communication with the quarry was established.

By noon, our line was as follows: Gird front line from M.11.c.2.1 to M.17.a.4.7 with a post in Gird Support line at M 11.c.4 ½. The enemy still had a post on the north side of Butte. We held Butte Alley and the Quarry strongly, telephonic communication with the Quarry still holding. On our right the 6th Durham Light Infantry had been held up by machine-gun fire and could not advance much beyond Maxwell Trench.

Independent witnesses stated that our advance was very finely carried out and that our men could be seen advancing very steadily. They passed right over the Butte and straight on to the Gird Line, where our artillery discs were immediately put out.

From noon up to 3 pm the position remained unchanged; the enemy delivered several determined assaults on the Gird Line, but these were all repulsed. Fighting still continued on the Butte, where we tried to capture the fortified dug-out on the north side.

At about 3 pm the enemy, strongly reinforced, again counter-attacked and at 3.30 pm we reported as follows: "We have been driven out of Gird front line and I believe my posts there were captured, and have tried to get back but the enemy is in considerable force and is still counter-attacking. It is taking me all my time to hold Butte Alley. Please ask artillery to shell area north of Bapaume road in M. 10.d and M.11.c as Germans are in considerable force there. Enemy is holding Gird front line strongly on my right, and in my opinion a strong advance to the right of the Butte would meet with success. I have a small post in a shell hole at the north-western corner of the Butte, but the enemy still has a post on the Butte on the north side. I am just going to make another effort to capture this post.'"

Desperate hand-to-hand fighting continued all the afternoon, and at 7.15 pm a message was sent back saying that the 9/DLI were holding part of Butte Alley and had a post on the north side of the Butte. The enemy however still had a post on the northern slope of the Butte, but the Durhams 'were looking to scupper this'. 'The Germans were still attacking and there is a lot of hand to hand fighting going on.' In a plea Bradford stated that, 'If another battalion were attached to me, I could probably take the part of the Gird front line'.

This story was not to have a successful ending. By 12.20 am on 6 November the attackers had been repulsed after a strong counter attack and all their posts had been captured or driven back. The Germans were still holding the dugout in the Butte and had attacked from there, throwing bombs as they attacked over the Butte, whilst the quarry had also been recaptured by the enemy. After heroic stands, the Durhams were back in Maxwell trench by 1.00 pm on 6 November, where they had been just over twenty-four hours earlier, prior to the attack. The 50th Division was now back in its original line of Snag, Maxwell, and Tail trenches. Orders were given for 150 Brigade to relief 151 Brigade, which was completed very early on 7 November (another attack, planned for the morning, of the 6th was cancelled). The action of 5 October had resulted in the 50th Division suffering thirty-eight officer and 929 other rank casualties.

The part of the 50th Division in the Battle of the Somme, which had commenced in September (for Flers-Courcelette), was nearly over; on 20 November the Division had withdrawn from the line and was in reserve. Before leaving there was time for them to play a part in another attempt on Gird Trench, Hook Sap and a newly dug trench, which ran parallel with Gird Trench, Blind Trench. Zero hour was 6.45 am on 14 November. The attack was unsuccessful; casualties for the operations from 14–16 November were another thirty-seven officers and 852 other ranks killed, wounded or missing. By the morning of 20 November, the 50th (Northumbrian) Division was replaced by the 1st Division in the line; all of its composite units had taken a severe battering. Its Memorial is on raised ground in the boundaries of Wieltje, north of Ypres – the Division first went into action here during the Second Battle of Ypres, which witnessed the first extensive use of gas on the Western Front.

The appalling conditions which the Fourth Army had fought during by the later phases of the Somme offensive were commented on by Sir Douglas Haig in his report to the Chief of the Imperial General Staff in London, dated 21 November 1916.

'The ground, sodden with rain and broken up everywhere by innumerable shell holes can only be described as a morass, almost bottomless in places: between the lines and for many thousands of yards behind them it is almost and in some localities quite impassable. The supply of food and ammunition is carried out with the greatest difficulty and intense labour. And the men are so worn out by this and by the maintenance and construction of trenches that frequent reliefs, carried out under exhausting conditions, are unavoidable.'

The mud had been as big a challenge as the Germans; it was truly the second enemy.

The Attack Made by the 50th Division on the Butte-De-Warlencourt and the Gird Line on November 5th 1916
By Roland Bradford

In the first week of November 1916 there had been very heavy rain in the SOMME Area and the surface of the ground was thick with mud. It was impossible to use any of the communication trenches and movement across the open, even right behind our lines where you were unmolested by enemy fire, was attended with great difficulty and was most exhausting.

The front line held by the 50th Division in that first week of November was MAXWELL TRENCH, which lay immediately east of the ALBERT-BAPAUME road and ran just behind the Southern crest of the small ridge on which the BUTTE-DE WARLENCOURT was situated. This trench opposite the BUTTE was separated by a distance of 250 yards, and throughout its length was an average distance of 300 yards from the German front line.

On November 5th, the 151st Infantry Brigade was to attack in conjunction with the Australians on the right. The Division on the left was not going to attack but was to co-operate with fire. The Objectives of the Brigade were the capture of the BUTTE, the QUARRY, and the GIRD Front Line on the left, and to capture and consolidate the GIRD front and support lines on the right.

Three Battalions of the 151st Infantry Brigade were to assault – each Battalion being on a frontage of three Companies with one Company in reserve which was to remain in Maxwell Trench. The 9th DLI was on the left, the 6th DLI in the centre, and the 8th DLI on the right. The 5th Border Regt. was in Brigade Reserve and was in readiness in the trenches north of EAUCOURT L'ABBAYE. The 6th Battalion N.F. was attached to the Brigade as a further reserve and was situated in the FLERS Support Line, just west of EAUCOURT L'ABBAYE.

At 9 am the assaulting Infantry moved forward. These troops were in four lines with a distance of 15 yards between each line. The 6th DLI and 8th DLI when they had gone forward about 50 yards came under very heavy machine-gun fire which caused them many casualties and prevented them from reaching their objectives, although many heroic efforts to get forward were made. The Australians on the right were met by intense machine-gun fire and they too were unable to make any progress. On the left the 9th DLI met with less opposition and succeeded in gaining all its objectives without suffering heavy casualties. The German barrages came down at about four minutes after nine o'clock. There were three barrages, one was a few yards in advance of MAXWELL TRENCH, the other was on HEXHAM ROAD, where Battalion Headquarters was situated in a dugout at the entrance to SNAG TRENCH, and the third was between HEXHAM ROAD and the FLERS LINE. All were particularly intense.

At 10 am the 9th DLI was disposed as follows: Four Posts were established in the GIRD Front Line the left one being on the ALBERT-BAPAUME Road. There were four Posts in the space between the BUTTE and the GIRD Front line. The front edge of the QUARRY was strongly held, and two Company Headquarters were situated in the QUARRY in telephonic communication with Battalion Headquarters. Each of the assaulting Platoons had a reserve Platoon in BUTTE ALLEY, the trench running immediately South of the BUTTE. Two Machine Guns were sited in BUTTE ALLEY and a 2" Stokes Mortar in the Quarry. Two Battalion observers were on the BUTTE. The Reserve Company of the Battalion was in MAXWELL TRENCH. Eight Bavarian prisoners had been sent back to Battalion Headquarters. Some other prisoners who were on their way back had together with their escorts been annihilated by the German artillery fire. The Germans were still holding a dugout on the north east side of the BUTTE. The Parties who should have 'mopped up' the BUTTE dugouts had either gone forward without completing their work, carried away in the enthusiasm of the assault, or had been shot by German snipers while at their work. The ground had been so pulverised by our bombardments and was so muddy that it was not possible to do much in the way of consolidation. But the men were ready with their rifles.

The Germans had now realised the scope of our attack and many of their Batteries concentrated their fire on our new positions. Snipers from WARLENCOURT-EAUCOURT were subjecting our men to a deadly fire and it was almost impossible for them to move. The Germans in the dugout on the northeast edge of the BUTTE had brought a machine gun into position and were worrying us from behind. Many gallant attempts were made throughout the day to capture this dugout but without success. All our Parties who tried to rush it were destroyed by the German machine gun fire from the direction of HOOK SAP and by the fire of the large number of snipers in WARLENCOURT. However, a Party did succeed in throwing some Mills Grenades into the dugout and this made the Boche more cautious.

The first German counterattack was made about 12 noon. It was a half-hearted one and was easily stopped. During the afternoon the enemy launched several bombing attacks, but these too were repulsed. About 6 pm the Germans made a determined counterattack, preceded by a terrific bombardment, and were able to get to close quarters. A tough struggle ensued. But our men who had now been reinforced by the reserve Company and who showed the traditional superiority of the British in hand to hand fighting, succeeding in driving out the enemy. The 9th DLI was getting weak, but it was hoped that the Boche had now made his last counterattack for that day. It had happened that the Bavarian Division which was holding the line when we attacked was to have been relieved on the night of the 5th/6th November by the Prussian Guards Division.

At about 11 pm battalions of the Prussians delivered a fresh counterattack. They came in great force from our front and also worked round from both flanks. Our men were overwhelmed. Many died fighting. Others were compelled to surrender. It was only a handful of men who found their way back to MAXWELL TRENCH and they were completely exhausted by their great efforts and the strain of the fighting.

There were many reasons why the 9th DLI was unable to hold its ground.

The failure of the troops on the right to reach their objectives and the fact that the Division on our left was not attacking caused both flanks of the Battalion to be in the air. The positions to be held were very much exposed and the Germans could see all our trenches and control their fire accordingly. It was a local attack and the enemy was able to concentrate his guns on to a small portion of our line. The ground was a sea of mud and it was almost impossible to consolidate our Posts. The terribly intense German barrages and the difficult nature of the ground prevented reinforcements from being sent up to help the 9th DLI. Four hundred yards north of the Butte the enemy had a steep bank behind which they were able to assemble without being molested. In the hope of being able to exploit success we had arranged for our barrage to be placed just beyond this bank. The terrain was very favourable to a German counterattack. Besides the splendid observation points in their possession the ground provided great facilities for the forming up of their troops under cover. At first sight it might appear as if the conditions were somewhat reciprocal, for we had the MAXWELL Trench Ridge, which gave us some cover. But it was not really so. The ground between the FLERS LINES and HEXHAM ROAD, before getting under cover of the MAXWELL TRENCH RIDGE, were very exposed, and the ground concealed by the Ridge was intensely shelled by the enemy throughout the day and night. It is wonderful, when one considers the difficulties under which our men were working and the fearful fire to which they were exposed, that they held on for so long as they did. And it makes you proud to be an Englishman.

On looking back at the attack of the 5th of November, it seems that the results which would have been gained in the event of success were of doubtful value and would hardly have been worth the loss which we would suffer. It would have been awkward for us to hold the objectives, which would have been badly sited for our defence. The possession of the BUTTE by the Germans was not an asset to them. From our existing trenches we were trying to prevent them from using it as an Observation point. The BUTTE itself would have been of little use to us for purposes of observation. But the BUTTE-DE-WARLENCOURT had become an obsession. Everybody wanted it. It loomed large in the minds of the Soldiers in the forward area and they attributed many of their misfortunes to it. The newspaper correspondents talked about "that Miniature Gibraltar". So it had to be taken.

It seems that the attack was one of those tempting and unfortunately at one period frequent local operations that are so costly and which are rarely worthwhile. But perhaps that is only the narrow view of the Regimental Officer.

This is a printed presentation of Lieutenant Colonel Bradford's after action report, the original of which is in the DLI Museum in Durham, and has been extracted from the Butte de Warlencourt Memorial Dedication Brochure produced by the Western Front Association in 1990.

29–30 January 1917: The Butte de Warlencourt set ablaze!

The 1916 battle of the Somme officially ended (so far as the British were concerned) in mid-November, the Butte undefeated, having seen off several attempts to capture it. The Département of the Somme was now in the midst of winter. By 16 December our friends who captured Martinpuich some three months earlier almost to the day, the 15th (Scottish) Division, were again back in the line in the area. One of the events during this winter spell was not the capture of the Butte but to see it spectacularly catch fire some six weeks after they returned, after a well-planned raid.

At the end of the year the opposing lines ran along each side of a shallow valley as can be seen from the extract of a trench map dated 1 January 1917. On the British side the ground sloped gently down from the ruins of Le Sars village, the front line being about halfway down the slope. On the opposite side of the valley were the German trenches in a somewhat similar position, and immediately behind their front line rose the Butte. The quarry close by and to the north-west was also known to contain dugouts, shelters, and trench mortar emplacements; this was also to form part of the raiders' objective.

From the British posts any enemy movement in the vicinity of the Butte de Warlencourt could be clearly seen, with the British snipers easily taking care of any Germans appearing in the open during daytime. Towards the close of the year snow, mist and the general Somme weather greatly hindered patrol activity; but in spite of this British parties were out in No Man's Land every night, and were successful on several occasions in taking prisoners and attacking the enemy's listening posts. In this winter period it was decided, however, to keep no soldier longer than two days in the front line, and to ensure that everyone had frequent changes of boots and clothing. Christmas and New Year passed by without notable incident, as also did most of January 1917. However, just before that month ended a meticulously planned raid on the Butte was organised by 44 Brigade and carried out most successfully on 29–30 January 1917 by B and D companies of the 8/10th Gordon Highlanders.

On account of the numberless shell holes and the condition of the ground, it was decided that the raiding party should form up in No Man's

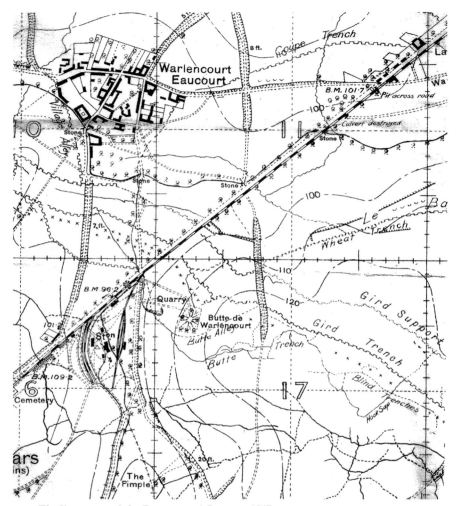

The lines around the Butte as at 1 January 1917.

Land and, as there was deep snow on the ground at the time, the men were to wear white smocks over their equipment and had their steel helmets whitewashed. Some of these over garments were ladies' nightgowns, bought in Amiens by two Highland officers, no doubt causing much hilarity in the shops when they informed the shop assistants what they wanted (not least because of the number required, it seems reasonable to suspect). To help eliminate any chance of confusion, black tapes were laid out beforehand, on which the lines formed up prior to the attack and, as was the custom on nearly all raids, the enemy wire was previously cut by artillery fire, in this instance the work being carried out very successfully. There was to be no preliminary bombardment, as the aim was to leave the enemy undisturbed until the raid started and give them no advance notice regarding the forthcoming possibility of an attack. At zero-hour life would be far from quiet. The adjoining divisions were instructed to simulate attacks in order to deceive the enemy as to the real point of attack, and the 15th Division's artillery, assisted by III Corps' heavy artillery, were to open an intense barrage on the German front line. This barrage was to lift after one minute at the rate of fifty yards a minute until it reached a point well behind the Butte and Quarry. At the conclusion of the raid, twenty-five minutes after zero, the barrage was to return to the German front line trenches, by which time the raiders were to be back in their own lines. Every imaginable contingency was provided for, and this care and forethought was largely responsible for the success of the raid.

At 11.00 pm on the night of January 29 the two companies moved forward to carry out this very daring and dangerous manoeuvre. Although they only had around 700 yards to travel, it took them two hours to do so without raising suspicions to reach their jumping-off positions in No Man's Land. By 1.15 am on 30 January the attackers were in position and formed up in two waves, each wave comprising two platoons from each company. On the right, Captain Match was in command of B Company, on the left Lieutenant Kenyon commanded D Company. B Company's objective was the Butte itself, whilst the target of D Company was the nearby Quarry. The tasks given to both parties were relatively vague: they were to take prisoners, inflict as much damage as possible and be back in their lines within twenty-five minutes of starting the attack.

Sharp to the second, at 1.30 am the barrage fell on the German lines and one minute later the two companies went forward. Practically no opposition was encountered except on the left flank, which was held up for a short time by a machine gun in the Quarry. On the right, just as the barrage lifted from the front line, two enemy machine guns opened fire, causing hesitation; but Captain Match gallantly rushed forward, followed by his company, and as a result the guns were very quickly put out of operation. On crossing the German front line Match's B Company discovered a trench mortar, which they destroyed by dropping a stokes bomb down its barrel and then ramming a mass of earth and grass into the muzzle.

Once past the front line, parties went forward north of the Butte to act as a screen for those detailed to deal with the Butte and its dugouts. On the left, D company had discovered an enemy outpost garrisoned by six men. These, half dazed by the sudden attack, surrendered without a struggle and the attackers swept on to the Quarry, where many dugouts were bombed and destroyed. On the right B Company was now investigating the Butte itself. Discovering several entrances on its northern side, the garrison was summoned to surrender. A few wisely obeyed, but at two entrances the reply was negative and as a result stokes and mills bombs were thrown down the entrances, which demolished the passages and which in turn trapped any enemy within. Twelve prisoners were taken, who were immediately sent back to the British lines; and the work of destruction continued. By a stroke of good fortune, a Stokes bomb that exploded at the bottom of an entrance set alight some tins of petrol. The resulting fire spread into the excavated recesses of the Butte itself.

By this time, the party had done all the damage it could, and it was time to return to the British lines. Twenty minutes after the raid had started the covering parties withdrew and five minutes later, as the two companies reached the safety of their lines, the divisional artillery barrage fell once more on the German front line. Looking back on the scene of their exploits, what they witnessed must have given the raiders great satisfaction as flames were now shooting out of the Butte, the German lines were being pounded, many of the enemy had been killed in hand-to-hand fighting, many prisoners were on their way to the compound, and not one single rifle-shot or machine-gun bursts were heard from the line they had just left. A prisoner, who spoke some English, told one of his captors that the dugouts in the Butte contained 150 men. Of these, twelve had surrendered; the remainder were, well, 'accounted for' by the fighting or the fire, which was still burning two days later. At 3.15 am the Butte exploded, throwing flames thirty feet in the air, the noise of bursting bombs and ammunition telling its own tale. Whilst they had inflicted severe casualties on the enemy, the party got off comparatively lightly. A second lieutenant was missing, and it is thought that he was killed whilst dealing with the machine gun near the quarry. Two lieutenants were slightly wounded, four other ranks were killed and ten wounded.

This was one of the most successful raids undertaken by the 15th (Scottish) Division. The raid had been well thought out, well planned and exceedingly well carried out, reflecting highly on every officer and man who planned and had the daring and audacity to take part in it; the highest praise was heaped on the artillery involved as the barrages were so accurate and destructive. The operation received serious praise from many sources, including from the 1st Australian Division. Two days later the 5th Australian Division began the relief of the Division; on 4 February the 15th (Scottish) Division's headquarters were at Baizieux, to the west of Albert.

It was now February 1917. The first attempt to capture the Butte de Warlencourt had been made in early October 1916 and yet four months later the Butte had not been captured. It had had men of the Durham Light Infantry on it fleetingly and it had suffered a spectacular raid and resulting fire; but it was still in German hands in spite of the best efforts of several British divisions. The German withdrawal to the Hindenburg Line was imminent and the Butte came, finally, into British hands on 25 February 1917 as part of the strategic German withdrawal to the Hindenburg Line. The Butte was back in German hands in March 1918, a consequence of their Spring Offensive; but this was short-lived and it returned into British hands in August 1918, captured by the 21st Division.

Hindsight is a fine thing and is not always helpful when reviewing decisions made on the battlefield, a battlefield which now presents a bucolic image, which – apart from the scarred Butte and the memorials on it, bears very little signs of the ferocity of the fighting apart, perhaps, for the nearby Warlencourt British Cemetery. It is very easy to refight an engagement with the benefit of hindsight and when the vagaries of war disappeared over a century earlier. Fighting in the area between Martinpuich and the Butte for much of that autumn was as much as one against the weather and ground conditions as the enemy. When you look at the Butte and the hectare it occupies it is surrounded by relatively flat fields, it is very hard to dismiss the view that the taking of the Butte de Warlencourt had become an obsession, a costly obsession; and one which accounted for a lot of men when the actual benefits of capturing it were perhaps, as Bradford argued, limited. Would the attacks and attempts to capture it pass a modern-day cost-benefit analysis; the answer would probably be no. Indeed, one must ask would any of the many costly local attacks in those truly horrendous conditions pass the same modern analysis? The answer again might well be no. Regardless, the 1916 Battle of the Somme was over, the Germans retreated to the Hindenburg Line and so we will leave the cost benefit analysis of these results to somebody else.

A photograph taken outside Warlencourt British Cemetery, c. 1922/23. The original is an example of the early days of colour photography. The Butte de Warlencourt is in the centre background. (*Albert Khan*)

Zur frommen Erinnerung
im Gebete
an den tugendsamen Jüngling

Franz Xaver Schmalzer,

Mayerbauerssohn von Piesenham,
Pfarrei Grünthal, (Grünthal),
Soldat beim 17. K. bayr. Res.-Inf.-Regt.,
5. Kompagnie,
welcher am 6. Oktober 1916 im Alter
von 23 Jahren den Heldentod für das
Vaterland starb.

Du hast gekämpft fürs Vaterland
Mit starker, fester Bayerhand,
Du bist gefallen wie ein Held,
Gott lohn' es Dir, der Herr der Welt;
Er gebe Dir nach blut'gem Streit,
Des Himmels ew'ge Seligkeit.

„Süßes Herz Jesu, sei meine Liebe!"
(100 Tage Ablass.)
„Süßes Herz Maria, sei meine Rettung!"
(100 Tage Ablass.)
„Mein Jesus, Barmherzigkeit!"
(300 Tage Ablass.)

Druck v. Hans Grau, Wasserburg.

Franz Schmalzer's 'In Memoriam' card. He was killed on 6 October whilst in the trenches in the Butte/Le Sars area. He is commemorated in St. Laurent-Blangy German Cemetery. (*Author*)

In pious, prayerful, memory of that virtuous young man

Franz Xaver Schmalzer

A farmer's son from Piesenham, in the parish of Grünthal [60 km east of Munich], a private soldier of 5th Coy, Bavarian Reserve Infantry Regiment 17 who, on 6 October 1916, aged 23, died a hero's death for the Fatherland.

You have fought for the Fatherland
As a strong, faithful and true Bavarian
You have fallen as a hero
May God, Lord of the whole world, reward you
May he grant you after bloody strife
Everlasting salvation in Heaven.

'Sweet heart of Jesus, be my joy!'
'Sweet heart of Mary, be my salvation!'
'Jesus, have mercy!' [300 days plenary indulgence in each case]
Translation courtesy of Jack Sheldon

A Guide to the Book and to
Visiting the Battlefields

The distance by road from High Wood
(Bois de Fourcaux) to the Butte de
Warlencourt is approximately seven
kilometres. The journey will take about
eight minutes by car or about ninety
minutes to two hours if going by foot.
The advance on the Somme in 1916, from
the start point just west of High Wood on
15 September, was to take two months to
reach the Butte, including the capture of
the settlements of Martinpuich, Eaucourt
l'Abbaye and Le Sars. The battlefield
covered in this Martinpuich to the Butte
sector amounts to approximately fourteen
square kilometres, measured on the best
map to have when visiting it, the *Series
Bleu* (IGN) 1:25000 map, *2407E*.

The northern end of the Somme
battlefield was no stranger to recent
battles. Prior to the arrival of the Germans
in the area in the autumn of 1914, there
was significant fighting here during the

Carte de Randonnée 2407E
Bapaume.

Franco-Prussian war of 1870–1871. In the first days of January 1871
Bapaume and the surrounding area was the scene of desperate attempts
by the French to relieve Péronne from its siege by the Prussians. There
is plenty of evidence from items found over the years that soldiers
involved in that fighting were on the Butte de Warlencourt. Nearby
villages, including Le Transloy, Biefvillers and Béhagnies, were all
flash points and the consequence is a number of memorials to that war in
the area. Sadly, but perhaps not unexpectedly, most of these memorials
are showing the effect of the passage of time, although the French
remembrance association, the *Souvenir Francais*, does sterling work in
maintaining them to at least a reasonable standard. The car tour includes

short stops at several of these memorials, including the splendid statue of General Louis Faidherbe, who commanded the French troops in the battle, which stands proudly in front of the Hôtel de Ville in Bapaume.

In 1914 the population of most of these Somme villages was small, some no more than hamlets, with the people largely involved in agriculture. However, from September to November 1916 these village names were to appear frequently on the front pages of newspapers back home in Britain: each insignificant place that was captured was broadcast as though it were of the first importance. I still smile at the headline of the *Edinburgh Evening News* of 26 September 1916, loudly proclaiming the recapture of the village of Morval, then – as now – a place with maybe a hundred souls.

The 1870–1871 war memorial at Biefvillers – note the prominence of *Souvenir Francais* at its base. (*Author*)

Of course this approach was not peculiar to the First World War – for example, nearly seventy years later the hamlet of Goose Green became a household name in the UK during the Falklands war.

The local people carry out their daily occupations in this special location. The cemeteries and memorials are part of this life and to which they show pride and respect, but one rarely hears the Great War being discussed, a war that one must remember was now over a century ago. The passage of time fades many a memory and interest. On the other hand, the last thirty years or more has seen a huge increase in battlefield tourism, to the extent that it plays a not insignificant part in the health of the local economy (and, alas, causes some annoyance, when the occasional thoughtless person ambles across farmers' fields when in crop or leaves a vehicle blocking a track). Even less is heard about the war of 1870–1871, a sobering defeat that rattled French national confidence. This was only partially repaired by the heroic defence of Verdun in 1916, some 270 kilometres to the south east of Albert. An investigation of the records of the wartime postal censor by Craig Gibson showed that the allied soldiers were welcomed (not least for the money that they brought with them); but the overwhelming feeling amongst French civilians was that they simply wanted the war to end and all of the armies, the British included, to go home.

The intense daily life of farming and growing crops dominates the locals' minds and the hours that go into these activities are immense. One notable difference from 1914 is the great decrease in the number of agricultural labourers, their place taken by huge, wheeled machinery. Another is that a good proportion of those living in these small villages now commute to work in the towns, working in factories such as Stelia Aerospace (Airbus) in Albert (whereas in 1914 many of the inhabitants of Albert worked in the Singer sewing machine factory). Drive the country lanes on a dark October night and likely all you will see are the lights of the heavy machinery engaged in harvesting potatoes and beet. It seems to be a profitable activity, judging by the amount of modern farm machinery and equipment that is often found behind a rundown barn, itself situated feet from the pavement, guarded by fierce dogs. Look past the machinery and you might well see a fine house; on the other hand there are also less impressive structures, usually dating from the post war reconstruction and showing few signs of having had much work done on them since. The visitor will rarely see sheep (I did once spot a pig, wandering up the road near Ginchy), but there are good numbers of cows. Thus the rumble of milk tankers, refuse collection lorries and different types of agricultural machinery, can disturb the peace and tranquillity of the night, particularly the early morning, in this agricultural area. If you are in a bed and breakfast or a rented gite, be aware of this rumbling; you have been warned!

Wind turbines are appearing in significant numbers, breeding by the month. There might be an end in sight to the growth in numbers, as the French President, at the time of writing M. Macron, noted in 2020 that parts of France are suffering from an excessive concentration of these massive machines, whilst a recent legal action has brought a halt to the expansion of numbers in at least one area of the Somme, south of the river. They have two benefits for the battlefield visitor, however. In what is a relatively featureless landscape, they help to plot your location today when trying to place it on a trench map; whilst the service road that each of the turbines requires gets you largely mud free to parts of the battlefield that were either inaccessible or difficult to access in days gone by. For many years the radio mast at Pozières (reputedly due for demolition) has been the reference 'jewel in the crown' for helping to place yourself on the battlefield along the Albert-Bapaume Road. For me this role has now been taken by the five turbines in a row that start near

Wind turbines seen from the Lesboeufs to Ginchy road, with Bouleaux and Leuze Woods in the background. (*Author*)

Sailly-Saillisel and those erected in 2018 around Ginchy and Lesboeufs. Using these as reference markers, it is striking to note how compact this part of the Somme battlefield is. Another incidental benefit is that the roads around such 'windmills' have improved in quality. This is a most beneficial development, which in places was badly needed.

What will soon be apparent to anyone who is new to the Somme is the almost complete lack of any signs of local inhabitants in the area outside the major settlements of Albert and Bapaume or on the main roads – and the part of the 1916 battlefield covered in this book is no exception. If only one had a pound for every time the question, 'Where do the locals go all day?', has been asked.

It has been a good many years since I first visited the Somme. Fuelled like so many others by reading Martin Middlebrook's 1971 classic, *The First Day of the Somme*; and armed with the excellent *Major & Mrs Holt's Battlefield Guide to the Somme* (including the most helpful map), the intrepid Paterson clan soon found out (like every first time visitor) that every village looked the same and that there were cemeteries everywhere. That first visit saw three attempts to find Dantzig Alley Cemetery, each one failing miserably. Places like Newfoundland Park, Thiepval, the Lochnagar Crater and the Ulster Tower were found without too much confusion and are probably even easier to find today with better signposting, not to mention the arrival of almost universally available GPS navigation. In the lead up to the opening of the centenary of the Great War in 2014, several of the local roads received a welcome overhaul and were widened.

We visited the Butte de Warlencourt during that first visit but found it to be a pretty much overgrown wilderness, seriously in need of some love and attention. There was little reference to it at other Somme sites: no mentions, no leaflets, no nothing about visiting the Butte. Seemingly the only response ran along the lines of 'What Butte de what?' and 'Oh, that is only the place where it ended in this, let us call it, central northern area of the 1916 Somme battlefields'. How sad is that?

Further visits to the Somme will likely shift your focus past the memorials and onto the battlefield. One starts to get a feeling for the roads and villages, helped immensely by a closer study of the maps, available in recent years in different formats and including much more accessible trench mapping. The 1:25000 IGN maps have also recently undergone a change, so that two maps, *IGN 2407 SB – Bapaume/Acheux en Amienois* [which includes 'our area'] and *IGN 2408 SB – Albert/Bray sur Somme* now cover the whole of the 'British' battlefield of the Somme 1916. These relatively new 'SB' editions each combine two of the old sheets and is a much cheaper option than buying the two composite sheets individually. There is also a very handy special edition 1:75000 map published for the centenary by IGN, *The Battle of the Somme 1916*. It is excellent for giving a general overview of the whole Somme battlefield, including rear areas of both sides and inclusive of the French zone, as well as extending north and well into the Arras battlefield, up to and including the north of Vimy Ridge; an insert section covers most of the 1916 battlefield at a scale of at 1:40000. These maps are usually available in the supermarkets in Albert and at the Thiepval Visitors Centre, as well as in the bigger *libraire* in both Bapaume and Albert.

Generally speaking, the further east you venture into the battlefields – say from the Pozières Windmill – and the further the battle action is from that associated with 1 July, the less popular the areas tend to be with the touring companies and the casual tourist. For me, however, the ground where the later Somme fighting took place is my favourite by the proverbial mile, in particular much of the area of the battle covered in this book, i.e. Martinpuich to Eaucourt l'Abbaye to le Sars to Warlencourt; and also around the Morval, Ginchy and Lesboeufs triangle. You might see an occasional car or bus, but the area will be very quiet.

When to visit?

Personally, I find that the late autumn and winter months are the best time to visit because there is nothing growing in the fields and you can see so much more. On the other hand, the daylight hours are fewer, the weather can be very cold and wet and the fields very muddy: you will need to dress accordingly. Be prepared to change your footwear when you return to your transport and have a plastic bag handy into which to put your muddy boots. It is a simple courtesy to remove your boots before entering your accommodation. Watch the interior of any rented car – do not return it covered in mud as you will get charged. On the other hand, the mornings in northern France 'start' later in winter compared to the UK. It can still be dark at 9.15 am, which is of course a perfect excuse for another hour in bed.

It is recommended anyone buying this book as an accompaniment to a visit on the ground should make sure that they read it first and make the most of the mapping – they should then have a coherent idea of the whole of the period covered by it and have a grasp of the key points, place and trench names on the ground.

Getting to the Somme
Travelling the battlefields without a means of transport is not easy – public transport is all but non-existent for many locations. However, cycling can be well worthwhile, although getting there by train can be circuitous – Albert is your best station. If you are thinking of using TGV check the web site (https://en.oui.sncf/en/tgv) for prices and deals.

By air
Most people come to the Somme by road, but some in the northern part of the UK and in Northern Ireland might want to make the most of their holiday time and are prepared to fly and hire a vehicle. Brussels, Beauvais (much favoured by low cost carriers) and Lille airports (as is the Lille TGV station) are well within travelling distance, but the most popular arrival airport is Charles de Gaulle (Roissy).

Car hire
Do not be tempted by hire car companies who appear to be at half price compared to others; they will get their money in other ways. I would recommend playing safe and sticking with the well-known names. It is the old story; you only get what you pay for. There are a couple of things to watch for when hiring a car. First, do not forget your driving licence, thoroughly check your car before you leave for marks and scrapes which may not be on the rental forms. If you see any marks go and see the renting company and tell them and make sure you take photographs of the car. Make sure it has an emergency kit. When returning the vehicle, at handover take photos of the full fuel gauge and of the interior and

exterior. These again are important as it is not unusual for 'sneaky' fees to appear on your credit card statement weeks later for cleaning the car or whatever. Whether you take the enhanced driving excess insurance is entirely up to do. On the odd occasion when we rent a car we do not but instead we insure our excess through Questor car excess insurance (https://www.questor-insurance.co.uk) for a fraction of the price; there are others who offer this facility, such as insurance4carhire.

When picking up your car make sure you fully acquaint yourself with all the dials and controls before you set off, especially those for the lights. From Charles de Gaulle to the Somme, allow two hours to Albert and exit the motorway at junction 13. If going to Bapaume or to points north of the Albert-Bapaume Road, take junction 14. Much of this journey is on the péage (motorway).

By road

Check the UK government's website (currently, in Spring 2022, www.gov.uk/foreign-travel-advice/france) for up to date guidelines for driving, health cover and pet travel. Motoring organisations, the AA and the RAC, also provide information on their websites. Amongst other things, you will have to ensure that you and any person accompanying you have over six months left on your passports (and that currently [2022] almost always from the date of issue) when arriving in France.

The usual car routes are via Calais or Dunkerque or, from further north in the UK, to Zeebrugge, which involves an overnight crossing. We prefer the Channel Tunnel as it is quicker and for us, with a dog involved, easier. Others much prefer the ferry and being able to sit back and relax as well as being able to walk around. If you are a frequent traveller using the Channel Tunnel or the ferries, check out what deals might be available for booking bulk journeys in advance; by doing so you can achieve substantial savings.

Ensure you have the emergency kit in your boot as required by French law: a warning triangle, spare bulbs, breathalysers, yellow high visibility jackets, first aid kit and so on. This kit is essential for legal driving in France (and, indeed, for most of the rest of the continent); it can be purchased as a package on line, or from retailers such as Halfords or the AA.

Make certain that you have the headlight deflectors required for a UK vehicle (and, more to the point, know where to put them on the headlights – it is not straightforward!). Many modern cars (thankfully!) have a simple switch/change on the menu to ensure that their lights dip correctly. At the time of writing, post Brexit a British driving licence is accepted on the Continent; but do check on the website, as it might be necessary to get an International Driving Permit. Remember that the old 'GB plate is no longer valid: you will require a 'UK' one.

You will need to get a green card from your car insurers – apply in good time, at least three weeks before your anticipated departure. I strongly urge you to buy European break down cover. If you do have the misfortune to break down on the motorway, park at the extreme right-hand side and phone your breakdown cover. If a replacement tyre for a hire car is required, be prepared to pay for it first, claim the money back later and be prepared for a long wait for reimbursement, if indeed the tyre is covered.

The normal car route from Calais to the Somme will be by the A26/A1, direction Paris; and exit (Junction 14) at Bapaume – it is well signposted. This is a 'péage' route, ie a toll road, so allow around thirteen euros a trip. It is far easier to pay by credit card; and note that many toll booths (such as the Bapaume exit) are machine operated only. One can obviously use the standard road system; but it will be busier, slower and will take you through populated areas such as Arras. On the other hand, such a route will put you through places which frequently appear in the BEF literature from the Great War.

Please be well aware of the PRIORITY from the RIGHT rule; unless your road is on a route marked periodically by yellow diamonds, or has a 'dagger' symbol, with the broader line vertical and a narrow line that crosses it, you should assume priority from the right. Often, but not always, such junctions are indicated by an 'x' sign. This means that traffic coming in from the right has priority over you – and sometimes cars shoot out at speed. Some of these roads can seem nothing more than tracks, but …. Note that the French very usefully, almost invariably in the countryside, not in built up areas, mark such junctions with white bollards with a red ring towards the top.

Accompanying animals

If you are bringing a dog, cat or indeed your ferret, there will be additional fees to be paid on the Channel Tunnel. On the ferry from Dover your animal will have to remain in the car whilst you are ushered upstairs to spend money. If you have a dog, apart from having a valid Pet Passport and an Animal Health certificate, remember you will also have to visit a vet in France for your animal to have tapeworm treatment within a fixed number of days before travelling back to the UK. Allow forty euros in 2020 values for a two-minute consultation involving an injection or pill. This procedure just cannot be avoided. We use the SCP Pouillade–Xemar, Docteurs Vétérinaires, 13 Faubourg de Péronne, Bapaume (Tel: 03.21.07.11.14) who have been first class and we have never had an issue. If the vaccination paperwork is not correct you will not be allowed on the ferry or train, so take the extra moments before you drive off from the vet to check that all is perfect. And, of course, post Brexit and with goodness knows what other changes that might be imposed, you must check on line well before travelling.

Accommodation, food, drink, shopping and fuel

The internet means that hotels, bed and breakfasts and campsites in the area can be sourced by a click on the search engine; almost inevitably there will be Trip Advisor and similar reviews of the accommodation. There are also sites like the Somme tourist board, https://www.visit-somme.com, and various publications which give useful advice. Note that there are several British owned B&Bs and gites on the Somme, in my experience of a very high standard; some offer evening meals. These are usually geared to the battlefield visitor market and are focused accordingly.

Local shops can still close for two hours at lunch time, on a Sunday and on *Fêtes Nationales* (of which France has a lot). On the other hand, thankfully, in recent years it is now usual to find supermarkets open at lunch – and of course the big ones also provide fuel at all hours (credit card) and most have some form of car wash. Supermarkets are seemingly everywhere. In Bapaume, Albert and Péronne there are Aldi, Lidl, Intermarché, Carrefour, and Leclerc. Be prepared for queues at the check outs, they can be quiet substantial (though self-service check outs are becoming more common). You will soon get to know the supermarkets and if you become a frequent visitor you will get a favourite. After years of using the SuperU in Albert we have now gravitated to the Carrefour in Bapaume. Some – most – supermarkets will open on a Sunday morning for around four hours. A good time to go is in fact at lunchtime, when they generally seem to be relatively empty; on the other hand, that often means that there is a distinct lack of cashiers!

Sadly, the days of bistros and cafés (people will look blankly at you if you try using your BEF French and ask for the local estaminet!) in villages are by and large gone. Nearest to Martinpuich there is (at the time of writing) the Calypso II bistro in Longueval. If staying locally in or around Longueval you can order baguettes there for the next day. It will normally be closed in the afternoon; and note that, after a hard day tramping the fields, if you turn up at 8.15 pm in the evening, fancying a quick half, there is a fair chance the shutters will be coming – or have gone – down; the shutters stay up until the last customer says *bonne soirée*. In the area covered by this book you will currently find places to eat, for example in La Boisselle and Pozières. These, however, are a few miles from the area of this book, particularly at the Warlencourt end of the D929, where Bapaume is in easier striking distance and where there are various cafés and restaurants which will also provide toilet facilities. If you have gone north of the Roman road, there are eating possibilities at the new-ish restaurant/tea room at Thiepval, next to the Memorial. There are toilet facilities in Longueval at the Calypso (assuming you have purchased something) and at the Deville Wood visitors' centre. Do not forget supermarkets and places like *Gamme Vert* also provide such facilities (but which, regretfully, are often closed for repairs/maintenance/flooding) as do the McDonalds, located on the outskirts of Albert on the Bapaume Road and near the entrance to the A1 auto route at Bapaume.

Chemists are common in the three main towns of Albert, Bapaume and Péronne and in all the larger villages – for example, there is a lovely chemist in Combles, a hundred metres from the relatively new health centre. Ensure that you have your own travel and medical insurance, cover in the event of serious emergencies. Take your own European Health Insurance Card if you have your pre-Brexit one; otherwise bring the new Global Health Insurance Card, which appears to have the same benefits. A doctor will ask you to pay for the consultation as will the pharmacy for any drugs. You then make a claim, quoting your card number, which may result in some form of reimbursement months later. The only claim that I have submitted took eleven months to be settled and for the mighty amount of forty euros. The local papers (*Courrier Picard, Voix du Nord*) will carry emergency numbers for ambulances, fire etc. – the standard international number is 112.

For petrol and diesel, the best availability (and price) is in the main three towns. The cost there will be much cheaper than on the motorways (worth bearing in mind for those with hire cars to return).

What to carry or have with you in your vehicle
If you are visiting in the summer, the weather can be very warm and so carry sunscreen, hats, and water for drinking. You will need good 'broken in' boots for walking if you reckon to go over rough ground. In woods (where permitted), wear long trousers: not only do they provide protection against nettles and brambles, they should also prevent you picking up ticks. The weather can change very quickly, so a lightweight waterproof jacket is a must in your backpack. Take a camera (making sure it is fully charged and that you have plenty of digital storage space), notebook (which will help you identify all those photographs of fields), binoculars, a compass, the IGN map for the area you are walking, wipes, a flask and sandwich and you will have

pretty much covered all eventualities. In the walking tours in this book you are never far from your starting point and in truth not that far from a cup of coffee or a toilet. Experience shows it is best to download and title your pictures every night and charge your camera battery at the same time.

Walking Tour One

The Area around the Butte de Warlencourt

Starting point: Warlencourt British Cemetery is situated 1.25 kilometres north of the village of Le Sars on the south side of the D929 Albert-Bapaume road heading towards Bapaume. Le Sars is approximately five kilometres from the centre of Bapaume.

Distance of tour: 5.8 kilometres (approximately).

Duration of tour: 2 hours 15 minutes to 3 hours.

At various points in the walk, it would be advantageous to consult the relevant maps in the narrative part of the book:
See pages xvi, 38, 49, 52, 57, 73, 76, 79 and 94.

Tour outline

Eaucourt l'Abbaye (modern day l'Abbaye d'Eaucourt) was taken by the British on 1 October 1916 and the nearby village of Le Sars fell six days later. After the capture of Le Sars the allied focus in October and November 1916 in this particular sector of the front was on the capture of the Butte de Warlencourt, located some 600 metres from the extremities of Le Sars.

This tour takes the reader around the battlefields of the Butte de Warlencourt, Le Sars and Eaucourt l'Abbaye. It is mainly on at least reasonable quality track, all of which is usually easily passable by foot; however, as one would expect, care must be taken in inclement weather when the mud has a glutinous quality that is seemingly unique to the Somme. There are no toilets on the route, the nearest – if it is open – being in the Carrefour supermarket approximately four kilometres away and at the end of the D929 in Bapaume.

An average walking speed of approximately 3.6 kilometres per hour (about 2.25 miles) has been assumed. The route is passable on a mountain/cross country bike; but walking is preferable if you wish to get the full benefit of the route.

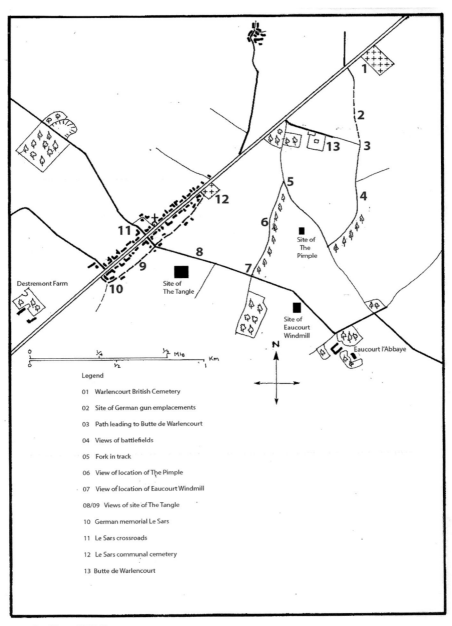

Outline of Walk.

Mud, mud, glorious Somme mud. Beware, it gets everywhere when the weather is inclement. (*Author*)

On arrival at **Warlencourt British Cemetery (1) (GPS 5547620/ 0485601)**, assuming you are arriving by vehicle, park outside the cemetery in the parking area, where there is ample room. Enter the cemetery by the main entrance. Always take a few moments to look at any information signage erected at the entrances of the cemetery you are visiting and look at the printed documents in the cemetery register box, usually located at or very close to the main entrance of CWGC cemeteries. Note that some small CWGC cemeteries do not have a register box, but this does not apply to those in these tours.

Pay particular note to the plan of the cemetery layout. These couple of minutes will save minutes of headstone hunting particularly in bigger cemeteries in the quest to find Plot I, II, or III or whatever (some cemetery plans have had the original plot numbers replaced with Arabic numerals). The layout for Warlencourt British Cemetery is shown here. Designed by Sir Edwin Lutyens (responsible for the Thiepval Memorial's design as well), this cemetery was established at the end of 1919 by concentrating original graves from Le Sars, Warlencourt and the surrounding areas. The largest burial ground moved into this cemetery was Hexham Road Cemetery in Le Sars, which was on the west side of the Abbaye grounds. Hexham Road (which gives a clue to the connection with the 50th (Northumbrian) Division) was the name given to the road

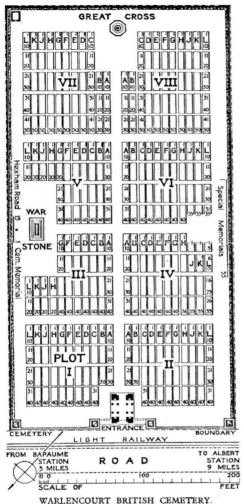

The layout of Warlencourt British Cemetery. Studying these plans is invaluable – in the bigger cemeteries almost essential – in finding a grave quickly. (*CWGC*)

leading from Warlencourt to Eaucourt. This cemetery was used from November 1916 to October 1917 and contained the graves of seventeen soldiers from the United Kingdom and thirteen from Australia. Given the size of the cemetery and the small number who were buried in Hexham Road Cemetery, it is quite clear that most of the burials here now were from very small plots, registered isolated burials or recovered by a graves registration unit after the Armistice.

A decade or so ago the cemetery underwent a massive refurbishment programme. Situated in low lying ground, it was prone to flooding and at that time heavy rains had left the cemetery stranded under a foot or two of water. It was clear that something had to be done and so a new drainage system was installed, the boundary wall more or less entirely dismantled and rebuilt and the horticulture was renewed. In addition, and as part of a major programme by the Commission that lasted ten or more years, all the Great War headstones on the Western Front – and indeed in much of the rest of the world – were re-engraved as necessary in an enhanced headstone maintenance programme, over and above the usual routine work. In 2021 this massive undertaking could be seen in the renovation and restoration of the Thiepval Memorial.

113

The cemetery now contains 3,505 Commonwealth burials and commemorations of the First World War. 1,823 of the burials are unidentified but there are special memorials to fifty-five casualties known or believed to be buried among them. Other memorials commemorate fifteen casualties buried in Hexham Road Cemetery whose graves were destroyed by shell fire.

Major Kayser was one of these fifteen casualties. Major Julius August Kayser (Hexham Road Cem. Mem. 6.) of the 12th Battalion Australian Infantry was killed in nearby Gueudecourt on 16 February 1917. Seriously wounded at Gallipoli, he returned to the front to be wounded again in July 1916 in the fighting for

One of the 'Hexham Road Fifteen', Major Julius August Kayser. (*Author*)

nearby Pozières. The Major returned to his battalion once again, only to be killed by a German mortar. He was 39. He was the son of August and Amalia Kayser and husband of Helen E. Kayser, of Franklin, Alberton, South Australia.

In III F.11 lies Victoria Cross winner Serjeant Donald Forrester Brown of the 2nd Battalion the Otago Regiment, New Zealand Expeditionary Force (NZEF), who was killed in action on 1 October 1916, aged 26. His citation in the London Gazette of 14 July 1917 reads:

'For most conspicuous bravery and determination in attack (south-east of High Wood, France, on September 15, 1916), when the company to which he belonged had suffered very heavy casualties in officers and men from machine-gun fire. At great personal risk, this N.C.O. advanced with a comrade and succeeded in reaching a point within thirty yards of the enemy guns. Four of the gun crew were killed and the gun captured. The advance of the company was continued until it was again held up by machine-gun fire. Again, Serjeant Brown and his comrade, with great gallantry, rushed the gun and killed the crew. After this second position had been won, the company came under very heavy shell fire, and the utter contempt for danger and coolness under fire of this N.C.O. did much to keep up the spirit of his men. On a subsequent occasion in attack, Serjeant Brown showed most conspicuous gallantry. He attacked, single handed, a machine gun that was holding up the attack, killed the gun crew, and captured the gun. Later, whilst sniping the retreating enemy, this very gallant soldier was killed.'

Brown was recommended for a Distinguished Conduct Medal but this was promoted to the Victoria Cross when officers of his battalion worked to get it upgraded to the highest honour. The award of the Victoria Cross to Brown was the first earned by a soldier of the NZEF on the Western Front.

There was an unusual burial in the cemetery as recently as May 2017, nearly one hundred years after the First World War ended. Private Henry Parker, of the 5th Battalion Yorkshire Regiment, died near Martinpuich on 26 September 1916, three days short of his 23rd birthday. He was commemorated on the Thiepval Memorial but ninety-eight years later, in 2014, his remains were discovered. Henry was buried with military honours

Serjeant Donald Brown VC, who died on 1 October 1916. (*Author*)

here (VI L. 36). The artefacts that were found with his remains were presented to the Green Howards Museum in Richmond. Although rare, it is not particularly unusual for remains from the war to be unearthed today, usually but far from exclusively associated with infrastructure work – road extensions and repairs, laying drains or services, that sort of thing. The CWGC and the Ministry of Defence takes their responsibility very seriously in these situations and go to great lengths to identify these remains and any surviving relatives; and, finally, to lay them to rest in an appropriate and dignified way. Since the early 1980s – for some years it was usual to remove remains to the CWGC cemetery at Terlincthun, north of Boulogne – the Commission has reverted to the post war practice of burying such casualties in a cemetery as close as possible to where the casualty was found.

Henry was the seventh of the twelve children of John and Esther Parker, who moved to Wansford in April 1896 after living in various villages on the Yorkshire Wolds. Thirty-six of Wansford's young men went to war and are on the Roll of Honour in Wansford Church. Four did not return: Henry Parker; his neighbour, Elijah Baggley, who has no known grave and is commemorated on the Menin Gate in Ypres; George Watts, who is buried in Bancourt British Cemetery, on the Somme; and Cecil Ullyott, who is on the Roll of Honour but is commemorated on the Harpham War Memorial, who is buried in Connaught Road Cemetery, Thiepval.

The lineage of The Green Howards goes back to 1688, when Francis Luttrell, of Dunster Castle in Somerset, raised a regiment in support of William of Orange. The regiment passed through the hands of various colonels until 1738, when the colonelcy fell to the Honourable Charles Howard, second son of the third Earl of Carlisle. It was under him that the regiment got its informal name. On campaign in Flanders in 1745 the regiment was associated with another, commanded by

Private Henry Parker, who died on 26 September 1916, was finally buried on 17 May 2017. (*Author*)

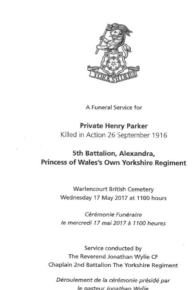

A Funeral Service for

Private Henry Parker
Killed in Action 26 September 1916

**5th Battalion, Alexandra,
Princess of Wales's Own Yorkshire Regiment**

Warlencourt British Cemetery
Wednesday 17 May 2017 at 1100 hours

*Cérémonie Funéraire
le mercredi 17 mai 2017 à 1100 heures*

Service conducted by
The Reverend Jonathan Wylie CF
Chaplain 2nd Battalion The Yorkshire Regiment

*Déroulement de la cérémonie présidé par
le pasteur Jonathan Wylie*

Private Henry Parker's Funeral Order of Service. (*Charles Crossan*)

Lieutenant General Thomas Howard. Two Howards caused confusion and the solution was to distinguish the regiments by the colour of their uniform facings. Those of Thomas Howard wore buff facings, those of Charles Howard wore green, hence The Green Howards and The Buff Howards, later shortened to The Buffs. It was not until 1920 that the historic nickname of The Green Howards became the official designation of the Regiment. It was as The Yorkshire Regiment that it went to war in 1914; it raised thirteen battalions and the Regiment served in all the major operations, in the process winning twelve Victoria Crosses. Some wags have suggested that the reason why the logical amalgamation of the Duke of Wellington's Regiment with the Green Howards during the reorganisation of the British army's infantry battalions from the 1960s

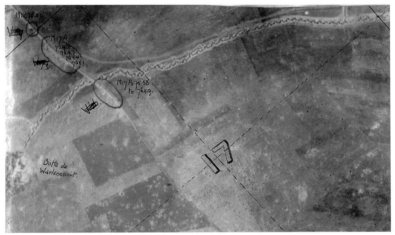

Original RFC phototograph showing Gird Trench and the German gun positions near the Butte. (*Author*)

The location of the German gun positions. The village of Warlencourt can be seen on the left in the distance. (*Author*)

onwards did not take place until 2012 (although not with the Duke of Wellington's alone) was because the resulting regiment would inevitably be known to the wider army as 'The Green Wellies'.

After your visit, leave the cemetery by the main gate. Facing the main road (D929), turn left and walk in the direction of Le Sars, visible in the distance. Keep to the grass verge as you proceed, facing the oncoming traffic. This can be a busy road, with a fair proportion of HGV vehicles using it. After 170 metres **(GPS 5547520/0485500)**, you will come to a track leading to the left. Follow the track, walking up a slight incline; the Butte de Warlencourt is clearly visible on your right, where you will be crossing over the location of Wheat Trench leading to your left.

After a hundred metres you will come across a line of bushes in a tree lined ditch. **(2) (GPS 5547300/0485550).** These bushes are the site of **German gun emplacements** that were used during the Somme.

Continue walking on the other side of the shallow bank (or indeed straight through it) for another 350 metres, crossing over the location of Gird Support Trench and you will come to a track leading to the right, with a signpost pointing to the Butte de Warlencourt **(3) (GPS 5547063/0485582).** This provides your first full viewpoint of the Butte, which will be visited later in the tour, and is the location of **Gird Trench. Butte Alley Trench**, which circled around the south of the Butte, met at this junction. Keep walking straight on and do not go along the track on the right. The cross marker at the junction of these two tracks is a normal location for battlefield finds to be deposited by the local farmers; they are regularly removed by *démineurs* and safely disposed of.

Such items are still regularly found even a century after the end of the war. Do NOT touch any items lying there, as they remain potentially very dangerous. Simply take a photograph and move on; a word of advice: if taking a photograph of such 'finds' it is sensible to take another photograph with some common object – a pen or pencil, perhaps – placed nearby so that it appears in the photograph. This is very useful for giving an idea of scale.

The 'Iron Harvest'. The Butte can be seen top right, the village of Le Sars top left. (*Derek Muir*)

Maxwell Trench and Snag Trench; Eaucourt l'Abbaye is in the centre distance. (*Author*)

Reaching the bottom of the track, you have great views toward the location of Pimple Alley and The Pimple. (*Author*)

Continue straight on down the same track with the Butte on your right, slowly disappearing behind you as the track descends. Please pay careful attention to this part of the walk and the following two stages as the ground conditions here in winter (and even in autumn) can be slippery. After 400 metres **(4) (GPS 5546650/0485550)**, halfway down the slope that you are descending, stop for a few moments to take in the view from here of the battlefield. In the fields to the left and right there are good views over the battlefield of October and November 1916. The location of Hook Sap is to your left and you will be passing over the locations of Maxwell Trench and the deadly Snag Trench. Eaucourt l'Abbaye is directly in front of you in the distance.

After some 250 metres, at the bottom of the incline, the track stops at a new track, which runs left to right across it. **(GPS 5546451/0485394)** To the left, which you are not following, it eventually comes out on the D11, running from Factory Corner to Le Sars via l'Abbaye d'Eaucourt. You will join this road at a later point in the walk.

Go right along the track; as you walk you will have on your left excellent views of today's l'Abbaye d'Eaucourt, which during the war was called Eaucourt l'Abbaye. Before the First World War Eaucourt l'Abbaye was a large farm complex, in existence since the French Revolution. Previously it had been, unsurprisingly, given the name, an abbey, of the Canon Regulars of St Augustine, founded in 1101 by a hermit priest, Odon. At the time it was situated in the middle of Mont-Oger Wood, part of the very large Arrouaise Forest. The abbey appears in a papal charter of Pope Hadrian (sometimes Adrian) IV (1154–1159), formerly Nicholas Brekspeare. He was, interestingly, given the activity of the BEF in the area, the only English pope. The Abbey was sacked in 1659 during the Franco-Spanish wars; the French Revolution sealed its fate and it was supressed in 1790 (the French equivalent of a 'Henry VIII moment') and its buildings sold off. Given its lengthy history, it is unsurprising that the buildings of the farm complex were so sturdy and provided the basis for such a strong defensive position.

The main attack on Eaucourt l'Abbaye was on 1 October 1916, by 141 Brigade of the 47th Division, assisted by two tanks. The shattered remains of the farms (in 1914 there were two farms within the complex) were captured by the 1/20th Londons. Six days later, on 7 October, the same Division attacked the Butte de Warlencourt, the first of several attacks made on the Butte in that autumn of 1916.

After continuing for a further 200 metres you will have come to the location of Pimple Alley, which ran across the track here. On your right, metres away from where you are standing, you will see a steep bank running parallel with the track. The bank on your right had to be crossed

The banking below the Butte which the troops had to climb. The Tail is just over the top of this bank. (*Author*)

by advancing infantry, with The Tail trenches just over the ridge at the top. Also, over the top on your right, are the locations of The Nose and Snag Trench. The ground on your left saw the advances on the Butte and is also the site of The Pimple.

Continue down this established farm track. After some 300 metres you will encounter a junction with a track that bends back to the left **(5) (GPS 5546822/0485153)**. Take this new track, the bed of the old light railway track that ran to Martinpuich. After walking in a general southerly direction for some 300 metres, stop. In the field on your left,

Another view of the location of The Pimple and Pimple Alley. (*Author*)

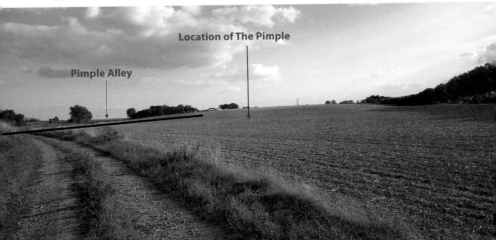

Roland Bradford VC

Roland 'Boys' Bradford, who won the Victoria Cross on 1 October 1916 at Eaucourt l'Abbaye. (*Durham County Records*)

Roland Bradford was born in County Durham in February 1892, the fourth and youngest son of a colliery manager. Twenty-five years later, when he was killed on 30 November 1917, he was the youngest brigadier general in the British army and the youngest in modern times.

Leading the 9th Durham Light Infantry into battle on the Somme in their first action on 15 September 1916, he was wounded. Sixteen days later, on 1 October 1916, here near Eaucourt l'Abbaye, Bradford led not only his own battalion but also the 6th Durham Light Infantry (whose own commanding officer had been wounded) into an attack on Eaucourt l'Abbaye and on the German trenches east of Le Sars. Under heavy fire, and throughout the advance, he ignored all dangers in order to lead and encourage his men on.

DEATH OF MRS. AMY BRADFORD

Mrs. Amy M. Bradford, who died at Folkestone on Sunday at the age of 91, was the mother of four sons, two of whom won the V.C., one the D.S.O., and one the M.C. A second M.C. was won by the youngest son, as well as his V.C. All four fought in the first world war, and only the eldest, now Sir Thomas Bradford, of Durham, survived, having been wounded and awarded the D.S.O. Three of the brothers served in The Durham Light Infantry and one in the Royal Navy. Their sister, Mrs. Bradford's only daughter, is the wife of Lieutenant-Colonel H. L. Cremer, of The Grange, Chartham, Kent. Their father was the late Mr. George Bradford, of Milbanke, Darlington.

The second son, Lieutenant-Commander George Nicholson Bradford, was killed at Zeebrugge on St. George's Day, 1918, his thirty-first birthday, in one of the bravest exploits of that memorable action. He was in command of the naval storming parties in Iris II, which could not anchor to the parapet of the mole because of the motion. A lieutenant who tried to scale a ladder without the ship being secured was killed on the parapet, and Lieutenant-Commander Bradford went to certain death by climbing a derrick and jumping on to the mole with the parapet anchor. He secured the ship and was immediately killed by machine-gun fire. His body fell into the sea and was not recovered. The V.C. was awarded posthumously.

The third son, Lieutenant James Barker Bradford, of The Durham Light Infantry, won the Military Cross in France, and died of wounds on May 14, 1917, at the age of 27.

YOUNGEST SON

The youngest of the brothers, Brigadier-General Roland Boys Bradford, also joined The Durham Light Infantry, and was awarded the Military Cross. On October 1, 1916, when serving as lieutenant, he saved the right flank of his brigade and of the division by an act of conspicuous bravery and leadership in attack, for which he was awarded the Victoria Cross. His battalion was in support when the situation of a leading battalion became critical and its commander wounded. Lieutenant Bradford asked permission to command the exposed battalion as well as his own, and by fearless energy under fire he rallied the attack, captured and defended the objective, and so secured the flank. He was afterwards promoted captain, then made brevet major, and at 25 was the youngest brigadier-general in France. He was killed in action in France in November, 1917.

The brothers were educated at the Royal Naval School, Eltham.

On more than one occasion Mrs. Bradford took her place at the Folkestone observance of Remembrance Day, wearing the two Victoria Crosses and a Military Cross.

The Times coverage of the death of the mother of the VC winning brothers, George and Roland Bradford.

In November 1916, Lieutenant (Temporary Lieutenant Colonel) Bradford was awarded the Victoria Cross for his actions. The London Gazette states:

> *"For most conspicuous bravery and good leadership in attack, whereby he saved the situation on the right flank of his Brigade and of the Division...By his fearless energy under fire of all description, and his skilful leadership of the two Battalions, regardless of all danger, he succeeded in rallying the attack, captured and defended the objective, and so secured the flank."*

In early November 1917 Bradford was promoted to the command of 186 Brigade. His extraordinarily promising career was tragically cut short, as he was killed on 30 November 1917. His brother, Lieutenant Commander George Bradford RN, also won the Victoria Cross (in April 1918, during the Zeebrugge Raid) and was killed in the action that won him the award. Roland and George are the only brothers to have been awarded the Victoria Cross.

approximately 150 metres away, is the site of The Pimple and Pimple Alley. **(6) (GPS 5546443/0485038).**

Continue straight ahead until the track meets the l'Abbaye d'Eaucourt to Le Sars road (D11). **(7) (GPS 5546270/0484950).** Stop, facing the road in front of you. Some 250 metres to your left, just in the field on the other side of the road, is the site of **Eaucourt Windmill**, which eventually fell to the British on 6 October 1916, captured by the 6/Londons of the 47th (London) Division. At this point you will have walked approximately 2.5 kilometres.

Look straight across the D 11, from the point where it intersects with the track that you were on and the one opposite, heading south. Look to the right of this track and about 400 metres into the field: it was in this area that Roland Bradford, destined to become the youngest brigadier general in the British army, won his Victoria Cross on 1 October 1916. Thirteen months later he was killed, on 30 November 1917.

Turn right onto the D 11; be wary of the traffic, especially tractors, and continue to walk in the direction of Le Sars. After 200 metres stop. **(8) (GPS 5546400/0484525)** On the left of where you are standing and approximately a hundred metres into the field is the site of **The Tangle** trenches, which were cleared by the one and only tank employed in the operation of 7 October to capture Le Sars. The tank was hit by a shell in this area and was soon destroyed; the early tanks, of course, were very vulnerable to a direct hit by a shell, even that of a field gun. The tank was very slow, even by the end of the war and especially when operating over shell ravaged country, which added to its vulnerability.

Continue walking towards Le Sars. Exactly fifty metres short of the main road, you will come across a track that crosses it either side of where you are standing. Go left, so that you are now walking parallel to the main road, heading west, behind the houses which back on to it. After a hundred metres, stop and look into the field on your left. Here is another good view of the site of **The Tangle (9) (GPS 5546300/048300).**

Continue straight on and after 300 metres, at the bend, stop. Seventy metres from the main D929 road and on your right you will see, behind a small farmhouse, a stone memorial **(10) (GPS 5546462/0484133)**. This relatively hidden memorial is a large stone block, the **memorial to the German 111th Reserve Infantry Regiment**. Commemorating 'Einen

The memorial to the German 111th Reserve Infantry Regiment at the southern end of Le Sars as it is today. (*Derek Muir*)

Left: The cemetery as it was in more tranquil days. Note the 'Griffin of Baden' standing on the plinth, all that remains today. *Right*: The monument after the end of the battle, most likely after the Armistice.

124

Toten' (our dead), the regiment's honours at that stage of the war can still be made out: Fricourt – Mametz – Montauban – La Boisselle. This memorial is illustrated in the original 1919 Michelin guide to the Somme, where it is described and pictured as standing in or very near to a ruined German cemetery.

Although showing signs of damage – it has lost the Griffin of Baden that used to sit on top of it, for example, the memorial is otherwise in reasonable condition. It is a pity that the visitor cannot nowadays examine it more closely. This is a very unusual survivor on the battlefield area of the Somme today that still has a major remnant of a German wartime cemetery. One of the survivors of the Regiment came in 1926, expecting to visit his fallen comrades here.

> I could hardly believe my eyes! The cemetery was overgrown but still in place. During the intervening eleven years the shrubs had grown large. Only you, dear comrades of RIR 111, were no longer there! Hidden in amongst nettles, as the sole remaining silent witness, was the base of the monument with its lovingly carved inscription *RIR 111 to its dead*. The Griffin of Baden in white sandstone, which once crowned it, lay smashed on the ground. Grief-stricken, I searched around to see if at least one of the gravestones, which had been carved so carefully by their comrades, was still there. But not one single little cross could be found ...'

It is highly probable that those who were once buried here predate the opening of the Somme offensive; their remains were almost certainly concentrated to the German cemetery at Villers au Flos, to the south east of Bapaume. Perhaps more distressingly, as Jack Sheldon points out in his *The Germans at Thiepval*, very few fatalities from the Regiment's fighting on the Somme in 1914 have a known grave. Of the 'hundreds during 1915 and early 1916 who died of wounds at the dressing station hospital in Flers, who fell in the fighting at Serre in June 1915 or at Fricourt itself on 1–2 July 1916, *not one single man has a known grave*.' When it came to honouring the dead of the war, it certainly seems to have been a case of 'to the victors the spoil'. This rather unprepossessing spot, just a few metres from the busy Post Road, with its rather woebegone memorial, overlooking fields which witnessed such fierce fighting in the autumn of 1916, seems a suitable place at which to reflect on the extraordinary endurance and heroism of the young German conscripts, for the most part, in those torrid days of September, October and November 1916.

Leaving the memorial behind you, continue fifty metres to the junction of the main road. Look left: in the distance and close to the

other side of the road stands Ferme du Château, situated on the site of Destremont Farm, which was taken by the British on 29 September 1916. Between Ferme du Chateau and where you are presently standing were two German trenches Flers Trench/Flers 1 and Flers Support/Flers 2. These trenches crossed the road approximately one hundred metres (Flers 1) and twenty metres (Flers 2) respectively from where you are standing.

Turn right at the main road, walk on the pavement into the village. After 330 metres you will reach **the village crossroads (11) (GPS 5546515/0484366),** this famous location being pivotal in the capture of Le Sars on 7 October 1916.

The crossroads was the scene of intense fighting in the capture of Le Sars. Under the guidance of Captain Denzil Harwood Clarke, companies of the 13th Durham Light Infantry, coming from the west, met with the 9th Yorkshire Regiment, who had stormed the southern end of the village. According to the *23rd Division History*, over a hundred Germans were killed or captured at this location. Clarke, when a lieutenant, had distinguished himself on the Souchez front (north of Arras) on 4 June 1916. Ultimately reaching the rank of lieutenant colonel, Clarke (who was awarded the DSO and MC) commanded the 13th Durham Light Infantry when he was aged only 22.

At the crossroads, take the road to the right, signposted Flers, Gueudecourt; after seventy metres stop. You are now back at the point where you joined the track running parallel to the main road behind the village. This time turn to the east, ie left, and proceed along the track, which is perfectly suited for walking. After 420 metres you will come to **Le Sars Communal Cemetery** just as the track meets the main road. **(12) (GPS 5546783/0484672).** Enter the cemetery by the side gate. The Butte de Warlencourt can be seen over the cemetery wall to the north east, some 600 metres away. Only one British soldier lies in the cemetery: Sergeant Robert Hinds, Royal Army Service Corps, who died on 1 September 1944, aged 32. His final resting place is on the right-hand side of the cemetery as you enter through the gate.

A hero from a later war. Serjeant Robert Hinds lies in Le Sars Communal Cemetery. (*Author*)

Leaving the cemetery, this time through the main gate, turn right and walk along the grass verge alongside the main road, again being fully aware of what can at times be heavy traffic. Visible from another angle is the Butte de Warlencourt, where the memorial and fencing on the top can be seen in reasonable weather conditions.

In 1916 the Butte was higher than it is today, and it stood, resolutely, overlooking the rest of the battlefield. The Butte was a chalk burial tumulus from centuries earlier; it is not too surprising to find such a thing when one remembers that the road you are walking on is a Roman road. Although several times in the autumn of 1916 British troops got onto the Butte, the Butte remained undefeated. It came into British possession at the end of February 1917, when the Germans retreated to the Hindenburg Line. Soldiers from nearly all the dominions of the Empire played a role, even tangentially, in the attacks on the Butte, with perhaps most prominence given to the South African Brigade and the Durham Light Infantry. The Butte, which is the last significant height before Bapaume, sometimes referred to as Hill 122, could be described perhaps as the British equivalent of Verdun's Mort Homme to the French army.

'The Butte would have been of little use to us for purposes of observation. But the Butte de Warlencourt had become an obsession. Everybody wanted it. It loomed large in the minds of the soldiers in the forward area and they attributed many of their misfortunes to it.'

Lieutenant Colonel Roland Bradford VC MC

550 metres from Warlencourt Communal Cemetery, you will come to a signposted, narrow road to the right. The signpost simply states, 'Butte de Warlencourt'. Go right and at the fork only a few metres ahead of you take the left road and carry on up the incline for 250 metres until you arrive at the **Butte de Warlencourt (13) (GPS 5547086/0485310)**. The clearly marked entrance gate is just past the car park. Where you are standing marks the end of the allied advance in 1916 along the Post Road, an advance that had started on 1 July. It is ironic that, in this section of the battlefield's front, the advance, which started in a crater some sixty feet deep, has ended at a hill now some sixty feet high. The advance during the Offensive along the road was approximately ten kilometres and took 141 days. This averages some seventy metres a day. According to the *Major & Mrs Holt's Battlefield Guide to the Somme*, this advance cost one casualty for every inch (2.5 centimetres). Arguably it cost rather more, but there again the British front was thirty kilometres long, so although it is a stark illustration of the human cost of the battle for the British Expeditionary Force, it has its limitations.

The track leading up to the Butte de Warlencourt. Amongst the trees on the right is the location of the Quarry. (*Author*)

The site is fenced but is always open. There is a well-maintained wooden walkway that takes the visitor to its the top. The Butte is now privately owned having been sold by the Western Front Association in late 2018 (they purchased it in 1990), as they were having serious operational difficulties looking after it. The well maintained, attractive site is particularly welcoming to visitors and benches are in place both at the car park area and at the top of the Butte. The benches provide a perfect opportunity to sit and reflect, in the tranquil atmosphere of 2021, on the contrasting scene in autumn 1916 and the ferocious actions that took place in this area. It is also a very handy spot to have a rest or a picnic. Enjoy the wonderful vista from the top of the Butte from where High Wood, Le Sars, Warlencourt and Eaucourt l'Abbaye, amongst other notable places of the battle, can be clearly seen. Informative boards are strategically placed and an orientation board at the top is most useful. The memorial at the top was erected by the WFA when the site was dedicated; take time to read it and reflect on its contents.

Entry to the site, as you would expect, is at your own risk and one must be prepared for the fact that the walkway is steep and can be slippery, although improvements are always being made. The handrails should always be used. The Butte has its own dedicated website (www. buttedewarlencourt.com), which is well laid out and very informative. There is also a section on it inviting people to engage with the Butte by joining the Butte de Warlencourt Association for a modest yearly fee.

On 3 November 1916, 151 Brigade, part of the 50th (Northumbrian) Division moved once more into the front line trenches. Three battalions were to play a leading role in the forthcoming attack. On the left of the Brigade front was the 9/DLI, under the command of Lieutenant Colonel Roland Bradford. In the centre was the 6th Battalion and on the right of the Brigade front was the 8/DLI. They were to attack the Butte on 5 November.

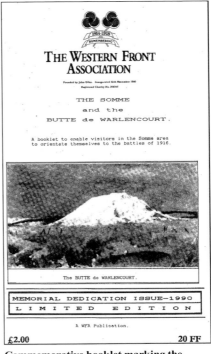

Commemorative booklet marking the purchase of the Butte de Warlencourt by the WFA in 1990. (*Author*)

129

Once the attack commenced, the only initial success came on the left, where the 9/DLI directly faced the Butte. It broke through the enemy lines and advanced over the Butte. The inevitable German local counter attacks began; just as Bradford thought the attacks were weakening, the Germans received yet more reinforcements. As they pressed forward, there was no option for the Durhams but to fall back from their hard won gains. Eventually the survivors returned across No Man's Land to their start line, where they re-joined their comrades of the other two Durham battalions who had retreated hours previously. The total casualties of 151 Brigade for the action were nearly 1,000 – that is the equivalent of at least fifty percent of those three battalions that were principally involved in the attack.

Bradford's comments written after the failed attack could have raised a few eyebrows.

'On looking back at the attack of the 5th of November it seems that the results that would have been gained in the event of success were of doubtful value and would hardly have been worth the loss which we would suffer. It would have been awkward for us to hold the objective, which would have been badly sited for defence. The Butte itself would have been of little use to us for the purposes of observation. But the Butte de Warlencourt had become an obsession. Everybody wanted it. It loomed large in the minds of the soldiers in the forward area and they attributed many of their misfortunes to it. The newspaper correspondents talked about 'that Miniature Gibraltar'. So, it had to be taken. It seems that the attack was one of those tempting, and unfortunately at one period frequent, local operations which are so costly and which are rarely worthwhile. But perhaps that is only the narrow view of the Regimental Officer.'

In April 1917, with the line now far away to the east, the 6th and 8th DLI each placed a battalion cross on top of the hill to commemorate the 5 November action. Another two crosses followed: a large cross erected by 151 Brigade and the 9th DLI added their cross. After the war these four crosses were brought back to England, the Brigade cross going to Durham Cathedral, where it remains today in the Durham Light Infantry Chapel in the south transept. A wooden cross was erected at the top to commemorate the German defenders; and two other crosses were put up at the bottom in memory of two South African battalions. There have been no crosses, however, on the Butte for many years.

And so the Butte de Warlencourt was never taken by the British in 1916. It was not until 25 February 1917, when the Germans withdrew

September 1917. The commemorative crosses stand proudly on the Butte; that of the 8th DLI is closest to the camera. (*Fonds des albums Valois* – Pas de Calais)

twenty kilometres or more to the Hindenburg Line, that it was finally occupied by the British. The Butte returned to German hands on 25 March 1918, during the spectacular initial success of the *Kaiserschlacht*; it returned to allied hands, this time permanently, in August 1918, when it was taken by the 21st and 42nd Divisions.

Leave the Butte and retrace your steps down the incline to the main Albert-Bapaume road. Just before joining the main road at the junction, stop. On your left is the site of an ancient quarry, now filled with trees, the contents of which no doubt helped form the Butte. Where you are standing is the site of Butte Alley Trench. Turn right at the main road, walking on the verge for 600 metres, which will bring you back to the tour's starting point, **Warlencourt British Cemetery**. It may be time now for a welcome cup of coffee or tea (or even a beer) in nearby Bapaume.

Walking Tour Two

Martinpuich and Area

Starting point: Martinpuich Church is located on the east side of the main street in Martinpuich, some 300 metres from the village crossroads from which roads lead to Longueval, Courcelette and Bazentin-le-Petit.

To reach Martinpuich, the simplest route from Albert is to take the D929, the Albert to Bapaume Road, often called the Post Road during the war. After some five kilometres you have to pass through Pozières; as you emerge from Pozières you will come to the famous Australian windmill memorial and the tank memorial, straddling the road. This marks, more or less, the start line here for the offensive that opened on 15 September 1916. Also here is a red and white radio mast that dominates much of the British sector of the Somme battlefield. It is easily recognisable from considerable distances away both north and south of the Bapaume road, which itself more or less bisects the British line, east west, of 1916. Continuing, on your left, you will pass the Canadian Courcelette memorial; almost immediately after it take a right turn at the crossroads, which brings you on to the D6.

This road, which becomes quite sunken as it drops down into Martinpuich, a kilometre or so away, was known as Gunpit Lane (or Road) during the war. If you had tried to walk along it on the afternoon of 15 September

The village church at Martinpuich: church spires are invaluable landmarks for today's battlefield visitors. (*Author*)

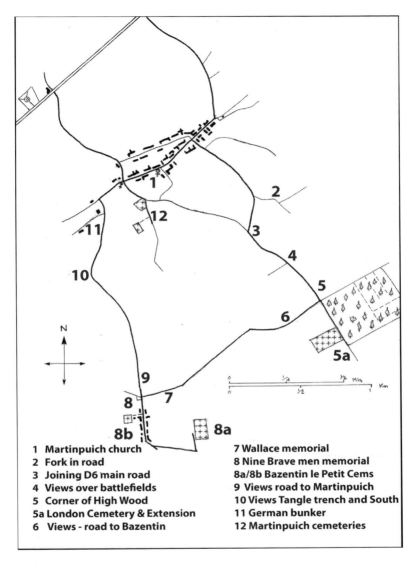

1 Martinpuich church
2 Fork in road
3 Joining D6 main road
4 Views over battlefields
5 Corner of High Wood
5a London Cemetery & Extension
6 Views - road to Bazentin

7 Wallace memorial
8 Nine Brave men memorial
8a/8b Bazentin le Petit Cems
9 Views road to Martinpuich
10 Views Tangle trench and South
11 German bunker
12 Martinpuich cemeteries

1916 you would have found that sunken part filled with dead horses, the corpses of German gunners and their destroyed guns and limbers, a scene of ghastly slaughter. Parallel and close to the right side of the road was the German Gunpit Trench. At this top end of the road the 2nd Canadian Division attacked on 15 September, the 15th (Scottish) Division closer to Martinpuich.

You will arrive at the village crossroads (with the infamous life-sized model cow on your right); turn left onto the main street, where you will soon come to the commune's church on your right. During 2020 the church underwent extensive restoration work, the consequence of which is that the spire is now notably whiter and acts as an even more effective battlefield marker than hitherto. There is plenty of room to park your vehicle at the church.

Starting Point: Martinpuich Church

Distance of tour: 6.2 kilometres

Duration of tour: 3 to 3.5 hours

Note: Walkers might find it helpful to refer to maps, pages xvi, 2, 7, 8, 13, 17, 25, in the narrative chapters.

Tour outline
Like the nearby village of Le Sars, the village of Martinpuich was one of the 1699 communes in France effectively destroyed in the First World War, a war that saw 633,000 French houses partially or totally destroyed. The village was captured by the 15th (Scottish) Division on

Martinpuich in ruins in May 1917: still a mangled mess months after its capture. (*Author*)

15 September 1916; it was lost in the German advance of Spring 1918, falling back into British hands towards the end of August 1918.

The tour takes the reader around the battlefields of Martinpuich. It is mainly along very quiet country roads, all of which are easily passable. Included are two optional extra walks, covering points of interest at High Wood and at Bazentin-le-Petit. Both these visits are covered in some detail in the vehicle tour, so if they are not inclined to visit them as part of this walk you can do so in that tour. There are no toilets on the route; the nearest are in the Café Calypso or at the Delville Wood Visitors Centre, both in Longueval (approximately five kilometres away) and both with varying and not always predictable opening hours.

This walk is exposed to wind and rain in places, with little or no opportunity for shelter. We strongly suggest that you check the weather forecast before you start the walk and dress accordingly. In wet, windy weather you may feel exposed at times. Walking is generally easy over these open, quiet country roads. There are some slight undulations within the **Extra Walk Two** to Bazentin-le-Petit that involve an easy to medium incline; and we stress again that care must take to avoid the occasional vehicular traffic.

Note: If the optional extras walks are followed, add twenty minutes to visit London Cemetery and fifty minutes to visit the Bazentin-le-Petit cemeteries. Again, the route is passable on a bike. Both these locations are, however, included in the car tour. Throughout we have assumed an average walking speed of approximately 3.6 kilometres (about 2.25 miles per hour).

The loggia, part of the 47th (1/2nd London) Division's Memorial in Martinpuich. (*Author*)

Loggia memorial seats to the 14th, 18th and 21st Battalions, London Regiment. (*Author*)

Park your vehicle outside Martinpuich Village Church **(1)** **(GPS 5544195/0483128)**, where there is ample parking space. Next to the village church stands a white stone archway (complete with battle honours), leading to a red brick loggia: the two combine (along with the

Martinpuich's war memorial. (*Author*)

wall) as a 47th (1/2nd London) Division Memorial, dedicated in 1925 and situated in the village because of the Division's magnificent fighting efforts in this area in the autumn of 1916. The school playground was also provided by the Division. Enter the loggia where you will see six memorial seats all dedicated to various units of the London Division.

The village war memorial is situated in front of the loggia. The Mairie (which also served as the post war village school) is situated just behind the village war memorial (near which there is now a plaque commemorating German Reserve Infantry Regiment 109). Take a few minutes to take a seat and admire how pretty this area looks, there are some wonderful photo opportunities to be gained here. As part of the funding for the centenary commemorations of the war, the CWGC received a special grant to renovate divisional and regimental etc memorials that are not their responsibility to maintain, at least apart from routine horticulture and patching. This memorial 'complex' was one of those beneficiaries, the major renovation work completed in 2014.

After your visit, return to the main street and turn right, heading north east. Some 300 metres from the Mairie and the Memorial, take a sharp right turn onto a narrow road **(GPS 5544351/0483350)**. Initially there is a shallow incline, but the road soon opens to give wonderful, all round views. At this point you are walking up a British objective for an attack in September 1916, the Starfish Line, which ran parallel just to the

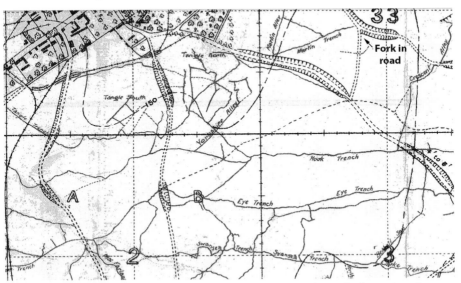

Your walking position at the Y junction fork in the track, marked on a trench map dated September 1916.

left of where you are walking. Further over on the left is the location of Prue Trench, running in a similar parallel direction and heading more or less east in the direction of Flers. Prue Trench led into the extreme, north eastern tip of Martinpuich, the area from which you joined this road; it was a final objective for the attack of 15 September 1916.

After 625 metres you will reach a Y junction **(2) (GPS 5543993/ 0483783)**. At this point you will have walked approximately one kilometre. At the Y Junction, the Starfish Line continued parallel in the direction of the left fork, heading over to the area on the modern map called Vallée Hugotte. Stop at the junction and look back to Martinpuich over the site of Martin Trench and, located across the road, the Tangle North.

Take the right fork and continue along the road, heading directly south, for 280 metres, when it meets the main D6 Martinpuich to Longueval road. Stop at the junction **(3) (GPS 5543702/0483758)**. As can be seen from the contemporary trench map, the whole of this area was a mass, indeed a maze, of trenches; no wonder it was so easy for individuals and groups of men – and tanks – to get hopelessly lost, especially at night and given the absence of so few recognisable physical features.

Turn left at the junction, heading towards High Wood, which can be seen clearly in front of you. Beware the intermittent traffic, which can move quite speedily: this road rates as 'moderately busy' by Somme rural road standards. After 225 metres stop again for a few moments; there is the stub of a track on your right nearby. You have reached an

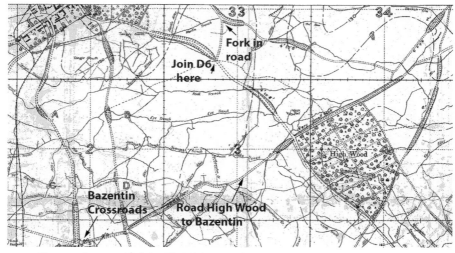

The trenches north of the High Wood to Bazentin road.

The view from the fork in the road looking over the locations of Martin Trench, Tangle North and Tangle South. Martin Trench is in the foreground, Tangle North was located in the centre left of the picture and Tangle South was to the middle left, behind the trees and bushes close to the CWGC cemetery. (*Author*)

important point of interest **(4) (GPS 5543557/0483950)**, where Hook Trench crosses the road. (It also marks the boundary between the Pas de Calais and the Somme *départements* – you are now going to walk into the Somme. To mark this significant boundary, the road number (currently) seamlessly changes from the D6 to the D107.) Approximately 250 metres further on you cross Eye Trench: it approaches the road almost at a right angle from your right (west) and at the road heads off into the field on your left almost directly north.

Continue towards High Wood; within thirty or forty metres, look left into the field to see the location of Vaux Post, which was the location of a company of the 4/Northumberland Fusiliers when 50th Division's

View approaching the north west corner of High Wood. (*Author*)

The impressive entrance loggia to London Cemetery and Extension. High Wood forms the backdrop. (*Author*)

151 Brigade was relieved, completed at 12.30 am on 21 September with three other companies located in nearby Hook Trench. Directly opposite the corner of High Wood **(5) GPS 5543131/0484241**), on your right, is a road heading south west Bazentin-le-Petit.

Tourers can take **extra walk one** by carrying on on the D107 for a further 320 metres and visit the imposing **London Cemetery and Extension (5a)(GPS5542955/0484419)**, which can be clearly seen from here on the right hand side of the road. This additional round trip should take twenty to twenty-five minutes; the time would need to be added to that given in the tour summary.

Enter the cemetery by the main gate, in the form of a loggia, taking the opportunity to read the cemetery register and visitors' book: a very imposing cemetery lies before you. Dating from September 1916, when – ironically – forty-seven men were buried in a large shell hole by the 47th (London) Division, an additional fifty-four graves were added to bring the total to 101 at the time of the Armistice. It is what is known as a concentration cemetery: these usually started as a small cemetery during or immediately after the war and were then greatly enlarged by the 'concentration' to it of isolated burials, of smaller cemeteries or of cemeteries that were too difficult to maintain. This cemetery, now the third largest in the Somme, was extended after the war and there are now 3,873 First World War graves, the vast majority of which (over 3,100) are unknown. There are excellent views across the valley to the west and the routes that the attacking British infantry had to take over the two months or so of frequent, morale sapping attacks on the wood until it finally fell on 15 September.

This cemetery was one of a select few – Serre No. 2 was another – where bodies were brought in from miles away, sometimes very considerable distances. This was especially so in the late 1920s and 1930s, after the majority of the cemeteries more local to where the remains were found had been 'closed' for further burials. Thus, for example, you will find buried here members of the Newfoundland Regiment (although only one is identified) who were killed on 1 July 1916 at Beaumont Hamel. Unusually, there are a large number of Second World War burials: at the far end of the cemetery, behind the Cross of Sacrifice, is a plot of 165 of them.

Captain David Henderson, who died on 15 September 1916, the first day of the Battle of Flers-Courcelette, is buried in Plot IA A.14. He was in the 8/Middlesex but was attached to the 19/Londons at the time of his death. He was the eldest son of the leader of the British Labour party at that time, Arthur Henderson, who was the first member of the Labour Party to hold cabinet rank, being a member of Asquith's coalition government on its formation in May 1915. He also holds the distinction of being the leader of the Labour Party three times.

Grave of Captain David Henderson. (*Author*)

The Rt Hon Arthur Henderson MP.

In 1938 a local farmer found the body of Lance Corporal Harry Woodfield of the 1/2nd Londons, who was killed on 17 September 1916; the discovery of remains years after the war was far from unusual, as the ploughs brought them up to the surface or work on drainage ditches or the foundations of new buildings exposed them. In his case what is relatively unusual was that they were able to identify him, in this case by his identity disc. He is buried in Plot 10 [X], which is to the right of the Cross of Sacrifice, C. 20. Buried next to him is Private George Hale, in grave C. 21; he was in the same battalion, killed

Lance Corporal Harry Woodfield's headstone. (*Author*)

on 15 September and found in the same grave; he, too, unusually was identified, this time by a stamp in the remains of his boot. There was another soldier in their original makeshift mass grave who could not be identified.

The road from High Wood to Bazentin-le-Petit. As an indicative guide, the 47th (London) Division were attacking from the left of the road and the 50th Division from the right. (*Author*)

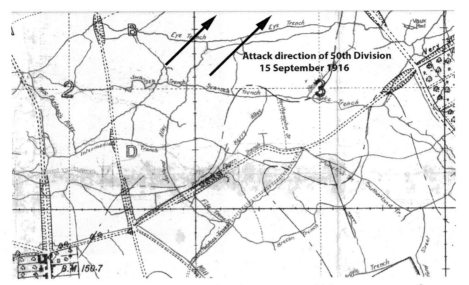

September 1916 trench map covering the area over which you are currently walking and the 50th Division's direction of attack on 15 September 1916.

Retrace your steps and return to **Point (5)**. [Note: if you were to continue a further couple of hundred metres you would come to the **47th Division's Memorial** on the left of the road, on the south west edge of High Wood. The memorial was originally rather more elaborate, with a stone surround around the cross. It was subject to subsidence – a reflection of the nature of the fighting here. It was completely restored in the mid-1990s by volunteers, the Memorial lightened by removing the stone surround to the cross, its foundations stabilised by pouring in vast quantities of concrete into the void below it and the paving re-laid. This extra visit **would add a further fifteen minutes** or so to your tour.]

Turn onto this minor road to Bazentin le Petit. After 250 metres stop **(6) (GPS 5542910/0483820)**. Clarke Trench came from your right, crossed the road leading up the incline on your right, where it then joined Swansea Trench. Further along the road, just beyond the point where a track on the right joins the road, you will cross the location of Intermediate Trench; and a couple of hundred metres after that, Jutland Alley. This trench ran more or less north – south, to the north connecting with Intermediate Trench, Swansea Trench (sometimes Avenue) and finally Eye Trench. In the fields to your right was the area of the attack of the 50th Division on 15 September 1916.

143

Continue for some 950 metres. Slightly hidden on your left, under a small stand of trees and by a track on the left just before it (which leads to the ruins of the well-known Windmill) is the **Wallace Memorial (7) (GPS 5542582/0483215)**. This is a private memorial to Captain HS Wallace of the 10/Worcesters. He was killed here, or very close by, in the attack on High Wood on 22 July 1916; his body was never found and identified. Born on 22 June 1892, Houston Stewart Hamilton Wallace was the son of William Hamilton Wallace, of Birkenhead. Brought up an Episcopalian, he went to Fettes College, Edinburgh, where he became a school prefect, captain of cricket and hockey and a sergeant in the OTC. He went up to Merton College, Oxford, in 1912. The memorial, which is an ornate crucifix mounted on a cairn and which was erected by his aunt, was refurbished by the commune, in part with the financial assistance of the WFA. For many years the memorial had been reduced to the cairn alone, overgrown with vegetation and with several of the inset letters missing. The crucifix and its surround was 'rediscovered' in a nearby farm. A service of rededication was held on 24 October 1994. Captain Wallace

The Wallace Memorial. (*Author*)

Captain Houston Stewart Wallace as an undergraduate. (*The Warden and Fellows of Merton College*)

is commemorated on the Thiepval Memorial. Wallace's was one of several private memorials on the Somme battlefield that were, thankfully, restored at about this time.

Memorial to the Nine Brave Men. (*Author*)

Continue for some 300 metres to a crossroads. The bulk of Bazentin-le-Petit is on your left. This village was frequently used as a forward base for units and formations involved in the later fighting for the Butte. Just in front of you and low down, in the angle made between a minor road/track and the D73, is a memorial on the corner. You have reached the 'Memorial to the Nine Brave Men' – members of 82nd Field Company RE **(8) (GPS 5542482/0482910)**. This memorial was refurbished in 1989 and again quite recently after a heavy truck went into it. It is to nine men of 82nd Field Coy RE who were killed in late July 1916. The names of the men are listed on the front of the memorial and on the rear is an informative plaque. On 29 July 1916 Sections 3 and 4 went on a wiring party above Bazentin-le-Petit, where they came under heavy fire. Knowing the work was vital, Lieutenant Howlett (with No 4 Section) and CSM Deyermond (with No 3 Section) carried on, although six men were killed and nineteen wounded out of the total of forty men deployed. Three men had been killed in similar circumstances the previous night; these nine fatal casualties thereafter were christened the 'Nine Brave Men'. It is an unusual memorial in that it was originally erected (at least the commemorative stone plaque was) during the war and it is specifically mentioned in a footnote in the Official History.

Extra walk two (NB! Note that this addition is covered in the vehicle tour in the following chapter.) This additional walk is just under two kilometres long and will take some fifty minutes to an hour.

At the crossroads/memorial to the Nine Brave Men turn left and head south down the main street into the small village of Bazentin-le-Petit. Continue through Bazentin-le-Petit, passing the church on your right and following the road around as it inclines to the left, for some 400 metres. On your left a minor road (Rue Neuve) branches of; follow this for about 300 metres; at a junction follow around a sharp left turn and you will see **Bazentin-le-Petit Communal Cemetery and Extension (8a) (GPS 5542194/0483328)** on the right and ahead of you.

The Communal Cemetery Extension was started immediately after the capture of the village and was used until December 1916 as a front line cemetery; this explains the irregular positioning of some of the headstones. In the fighting around 14 July, during which period the village was captured, there was an advanced dressing station close by and it was to there that the very badly wounded Robert Graves was brought whilst serving with the Royal Welsh Fusiliers: it was the end of his active service in France.

The cemetery was enlarged after the Armistice when fifty graves were brought in from the battlefields around Bazentin and Contalmaison. It now contains 185 burials and commemorations from the First World War; fifty-three of the burials are unidentified and fifty-nine (mainly from the 1st Northamptons) destroyed by shell fire are now represented by special memorials.

Bazentin Communal Cemetery Extension. (*Author*)

The entrance to Bazentin-le-Petit Military Cemetery; note the use of barbed wire pickets in the fencing. (*Author*)

One British soldier was reburied in this cemetery from Sailly-Laurette German Cemetery when the 556 German burials in that cemetery were removed after the war. This is a clear example of the distances that remains could be moved when it came to a reburial and also illustrates the often puzzling location of these casualties' final resting place. The shortest distance by road between the two locations is over twenty kilometres and the vehicle bringing the remains must have passed by literally tens of CWGC cemeteries to get to this one. Other examples of this puzzling situation include men of the Newfoundland Regiment killed on 1 July 1916 who are now buried south of Péronne!

Special memorials are erected to various soldiers whose graves in turn became victims of the war, destroyed by shell fire and subsequent fighting. Next to the extension is the Communal Cemetery; there are two British graves on either side of the main grass path. These men were from the Loyal North Lancs and Gloucestershire regiments.

Retrace your steps to the main street and turn right, heading back up the main village street towards the crossroads. After about 180 metres you will see a distinctive CWGC signpost on your left, indicating **Bazentin**

Captain Harold Oscar Teague.   Captain Teague's headstone and unusual
(*Brighton Grammar, Victoria*)   tribute. (*Author*)

le Petit Military Cemetery (8b) (GPS 5542276/0482927). Walk up the approach lane to the cemetery, noting the interesting salvaged pickets from the war lining the pathway. Be aware that the access path is often muddy and slippery in poor weather.

Buried in grave G.11 is Captain Harold Oscar Teague, who was killed, aged 39, on 14 February 1917. Teague was a doctor who was attached to the 11th Battalion AIF (Australian Imperial Force). Mentioned in Despatches, he was the son of John Henry and Elizabeth Teague and a native of Bendigo, Victoria, Australia. What is unusual is that beside his head stone is a private memorial: 'In Loving Memory of the late Captain H. O. Teague. Killed in action on 14 February 1917, as a token of love and admiration from the NCOs and men of the Australian Field Ambulance.'

Return to the road. Turn left and head back to the Nine Brave Men Memorial, which you will reach after 200 metres. **Extra Walk 2 ends here**.

At the crossroads, leaving the Memorial on your left, go straight over the crossroads to the minor road heading to Martinpuich. This is a very quiet country road but traffic does use it; be aware of vehicles, something of which we have to be increasingly aware with the growing use of electrically powered vehicles. After about 400 metres, stop. You have reached the site of **6th Avenue Trench (9) (GPS 5542748/0482906)**, which ran across the road here; it linked up to Lancashire Trench, which ran off to your left a few metres in front of you. Continuing your walk, you will soon pass the locations of, first, 70th Avenue on your left and, about 100 metres after a left incline in the road, Sanderson

A view of Martinpuich from the south east. (*Author*)

Trench; shortly the buildings of Martinpuich will come into view. As an approximate guide you are walking on a divisional boundary for the attack of 15 September 1916. The 15th (Scottish) Division attacked Martinpuich from the fields on your left. Closest to you on your left was 45 Brigade and beyond them 46 Brigade. The left flank of the 50th (Northumbrian) Division advanced from your right towards the area at the bottom, southern end of the village. Closest to you on your left was 45 Brigade and beyond them 46 Brigade.

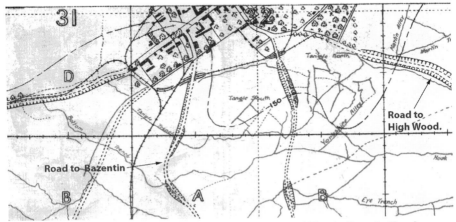

Trench map dated 29 September showing location of Tangle Trench, Tangle South and, on the right, Tangle North.

As you progress along the road, again on your left, you pass the sites of jumping off trenches that gloried in innocuous sounding names such as Bacon and Egg, followed a hundred metres or so in front of these by Ham and Liver. Bottom Trench ran across the road more or less where it bends back to the right. After some 750 metres, stop: this is the area of **Tangle Trench and Tangle South (10) (GPS 5543583/0482689).** Tangle Trench crosses the road here and goes into the field on the right; Tangle South was located approximately 400 metres to the north east, very close to the CWGC cemetery, which can be seen from here.

Continue heading north for 275 metres. As you are coming into the village, on your far left-hand side across the fields, is the location of the Sunken Road (under the letter 'D' on the extract from the trench map); slightly further on there is a minor road and almost immediately on its right side is a well-known **German bunker (11) (GPS 5543894/0482735).** Stop here. In recent years it has been made accessible to the public; it is now possible to walk around the outside of and enter into this extensive (for the Somme) bunker. Note the number of wire pickets that have been used here; they are a reasonably common sight along agricultural fence lines on the Somme. We should be grateful to the landowner for making the bunker accessible, one of the very few that exist in the 'British' sector of the Somme battlefield and of the even fewer that date to before 1 July 1916. There are a number of reasons why there is such a paucity

The accessible, impressive German bunker at Martinpuich, probably originally a regimental HQ. (*Author*)

Martinpuich British Cemetery. Approximately a hundred metres behind the Cross of Sacrifice is the location of Tangle South. (*Author*)

of concrete workings on the Somme battlefield; one is that it was very easy to work in the chalk, never far below the surface, and which was an adequately stable material into which to excavate. What bunkers there are tend to date to 1918, when the Germans returned to this area once more; and it is certainly a far cry from the significant number of concrete remnants to be found in the Hindenburg Line before Cambrai.

This minor road served as the inter brigade boundary for the 15th (Scottish) Division for the attack on 15 September 1916.

Return to the Bazentin road and turn left for the remaining short walk into Martinpuich. Note that when you come to the T junction the Factory Line came out here more or less directly opposite you; from here it ran north westwards to the Albert-Bapaume Road. Turn right onto the main road (Grande Rue) that runs through the village; after 200 metres, at the crossroads, turn right, taking the D6 that leads to Longueval. Walk a further 200 metres and you will see the signs for **Martinpuich Communal and Martinpuich British cemeteries (12) (GPS 5543950/0483000 and 5543810/0482929)** cemeteries. We will visit Martinpuich British Cemetery first, passing the village cemetery en route.

Martinpuich British Cemetery was started in November 1916 and used by fighting units and field ambulances until June the following year; it reopened at the end of August 1918, when the area was recaptured from the Germans. Nearly all those buried here, therefore, were killed in the period from right at the end of the Battle of the Somme to the German withdrawal to the Hindenburg Line. Holding the line in the ghastly conditions of the winter of 1916–1917 would have been bad enough on a quiet part of the line; here the British trenches were exposed and the communications and supply line ran over almost impossible ground conditions.

In 1931 the bodies of ten soldiers buried by the Germans were found in the communal cemetery (possibly moved there when the French were clearing the two German Martinpuich cemeteries soon after the end of the war?) and moved into the British Cemetery. Among them were Second Lieutenant Noel Blakeway, Lance Corporal Alfred May, Private Francis Fielding and Private Janes Gallivan, all of 1/Dorsets, who were killed on 27 March 1916 in the course of a German raid on Y Sap, at the southern end of La Boisselle. There is one RAF burial (the RAF was created on 1 April 1918): Second Lieutenant William Seller of 98 Squadron was shot down on 29 August 1918 whilst flying a DH9. The cemetery now contains 115 burials and commemorations of the First World War. Nine of the burials are unidentified and four graves were destroyed by shell fire in 1918 and the soldiers concerned are now represented by special memorials. Good views of the battlefield to the west can be had from the high ground behind the Cross of Sacrifice.

The Germans had two cemeteries in Martinpuich, No 1 and, unsurprisingly, No 2, which were situated quite close together at the

One of the Martinpuich German Military cemeteries. (*Fonds des albums Valois – Pas-de-Calais*).

Martinpuich Communal Cemetery. (*Author's collection*)

north eastern end of the village. As happened to almost every German cemetery associated with the 1916 Somme line (and there were a lot of them), fairly early in the post war years these cemeteries were destroyed, the remains were removed with varying degrees of care and were concentrated to a very limited number of sites, the biggest of which are at Fricourt, Rancourt and, south of the river, Vermandovillers.

Now walk back to Martinpuich Communal Cemetery. It contains five burials of the Great War, one of which is unidentified; two have their own headstone and two are commemorated on a special memorial; the fifth is unknown.

French communal cemeteries are sometimes not the prettiest of places and, in common with many of them, a number of the local graves in the cemetery, due to their poor and in places dangerous condition, were being reclaimed by the authorities in 2020. It is, perhaps, an interesting reflection on social change, even in a deeply rural area like this. Decades ago the same families would live in the same place for generations; now there is the pull of the town and, in any case, the traditional local employment has been radically changed through mechanisation. Still, in 1896 the population was 620; shortly before the war it was 500 or so; and now it is about 200.

The Martinpuich crossroads cow that misses nobody. Entrance at the cow's discretion. (*Author*)

Retrace your steps to the village crossroads, where you can admire the slightly startled looking model cow: perhaps it might be a cunning speed trap/hidden traffic camera? There again, perhaps not. Turn right and, after 300 metres, you will be back at **Martinpuich Church (1) (GPS 554495/0483128)**, your vehicle and the end of Walk Two.

Touring the area by vehicle

Behind the German Lines

Starting point: Bazentin Communal Extension Cemetery, Bazentin-le-Petit.

Distance of tour: Approximately fifty kilometres.

Duration of tour: Varying, depending on type of vehicle used and time spent at points of interest. If the most is made of the various stops and the tour is one go, it would be best to give it a full day.

Tour outline: A tour by vehicle (by this is meant a car or a medium sized minibus; anything bigger would need a reconnaissance first to assess the suitability of routes and the accessibility of some of the locations). The route does not require a vehicle with 4x4 capability.

The tour starts in Bazentin-le-Petit and ends at the Butte de Warlencourt; it may be split into two parts, with Bapaume acting as the end of Part 1 and the start of Part 2.

Bazentin-le-Petit – High Wood – Martinpuich – Courcelette – Le Sars – l'Abbaye d'Eaucourt (Eaucourt l'Abbaye) – Le Barque/Ligny Thilloy – Bapaume (including stop for coffee, lunch) – Avesnes lès Bapaume – Favreuil – Sapignies – Béhagnies – Achiet le Grand – Biefvillers (lès-Bapaume) – Grévillers – Warlencourt – Butte de Warlencourt.

This tour by vehicle will take in many of the perhaps lesser visited sites of the Le Sars and Bapaume sectors of the Battle of the Somme. The itinerary also includes some of the area's memorials relating to actions of the 1870–1871 Franco-Prussian War.

As the tour contains twenty-nine points of interest of various shapes and extent, if the reader so wishes this tour can be accomplished in two parts, part one being from Bazentin-le Petit to Bapaume, part two from Bapaume to the Butte de Warlencourt. We also recommend reading Walking Tours 1 and 2 for extra information at the appropriate locations.

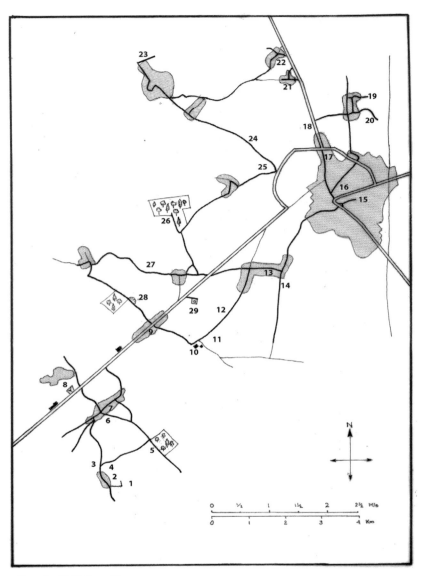

Tour by Vehicle outline map.

The starting point is in the sleepy village of **Bazentin-le-Petit**, situated on the D73 and approximately eleven kilometres north east of Albert. It was in German hands until 14 July 1916, when the 3rd and 7th Divisions recaptured the village. The village fell again in early Spring 1918 during

Vehicle Tour Map Key
1. Bazentin-le-Petit Communal Cemetery and Extension
2. Bazentin-le-Petit Military Cemetery
3. Memorial to the Nine Brave Men
4. Private Memorial to Captain Houston Hamilton
5. London Cemetery and Extension
6. Martinpuich Communal and Military Cemeteries
7. Martinpuich Church and 47th (London) Division Loggia
8. Canadian Memorial
9. Le Sars village crossroads
10. L'Abbaye d'Eaucourt
11. Le Barque road
12. View over the area of Hook Sap
13. Major Lanoe Hawker VC Memorial
14. Ligny-Thilloy Communal Cemetery
15. Bapaume Australian Cemetery
16. Monument to General Louis Faidherbe
17. Bapaume Communal Cemetery
18. Memorial to the 1870–1871 Franco-Prussian Battle of Bapaume
19. Communal Cemetery in Favreuil
20. Favreuil British Cemetery
21. Sapignies German Cemetery
22. Béhagnies Church 1870–1871 Monument
23. Achiet-le-Grand Communal Cemetery Extension
24. Biefvillers-lès-Bapaume 1870–1871 War Memorial
25. Grévillers Military Cemetery
26. Memorial and VC commemoration to Oswald Wainwright
27. The site of German Gun Emplacements
28. Le Sars Quarry
29. Butte de Warlencourt

the first of great German 1918 offensives on the Western Front: it was recaptured on 25 August 1918 by the 38th (Welsh) Division: ironic, as it is this division that is so closely allied with the desperate fighting in nearby Mametz Wood in July 1916.

In *Walk Two*, we reached the crossroads at the top of the village of Bazentin-le-Petit; however, unless you carried out the *Second Extra Walk*, you did not see the rarely visited cemeteries in the village. This is now your chance so to do.

Bazentin-le-Petit Communal Cemetery Extension. (*Author*)

Start your tour by parking your vehicle outside **Bazentin-le-Petit Communal Cemetery and Extension (1) (GPS 5542198/0483330)**. This very quiet cemetery is situated in an eastern valley off Rue Lamarck, the road which runs through the village, signposted at the corner of Rue Neuve, which is diagonally opposite the church. The cemetery is approximately 500 metres from this signpost, with good parking at its front at the end of an easy access road. As for all CWGC cemetery visits, we recommend making the most of the registers found in all but the smallest of these cemeteries.

The Communal Cemetery Extension started immediately after the capture of the village and was used until December 1916 as a front-line cemetery. It was enlarged after the Armistice when fifty graves were brought in from the battlefields of Bazentin and Contalmaison. It now contains 185 burials and commemorations of the Great War. Fifty-three of the burials are unidentified and fifty-nine (mainly of the 1st Northamptons) destroyed by shell fire are now represented by special memorials.

Captain Thomas Baxter Handyside Rorie
Captain Thomas Handyside Baxter Rorie, buried in plot J.2, of the 1/4th Black Watch, was attached to the 10/Glosters and was killed on 18 August 1916, aged 41. The son of Dr and Mrs James Rorie, husband of

Blanche Rorie and father of one child, his local newspaper, *The Courier*, described Captain Rorie 'as a splendid sportsman, and a thorough gentleman and when the sad event became known throughout the city of Dundee many were the expressions of regret by those who had known the captain, whether as a soldier, in business, or in sporting circles. His pleasing personality had won him friends wherever he went.' Captain Rorie, who was a chartered accountant in Dundee, was aged 41, the elder surviving son of Dr James Rorie, formerly medical superintendent at Westgreen Asylum.

After being admitted a member of the Glasgow Chartered Accountants' Society in 1897 he started business on his own account in Dundee. He joined the Black Watch shortly after

Captain Thomas Baxter Handyside Rorie (left) seated beside his brother. (*Rorie family records*)

Captain Rorie's grave in Bazentin-le-Petit Communal Cemetery Extension. (*Author*)

Captain Rorie's name on the High School of Dundee WW1 Roll of Honour. (*Courtesy High School of Dundee*)

war broke out and was attached to the Glosters before he was killed near Contalmaison. In business Captain Rorie held several public appointments, including carrying out audits for the Scottish Office and the Local Government Board, and was auditor of the Dundee Corporation gas accounts and the Common Good account. He was a member of several public bodies, which included the Parish Council, the Harbour Trust, and the Dundee District Committee of the Forfar County Council. In sporting circles he was well known as a cricketer, being a member of the Forfarshire and the Grange clubs. He was also a supporter of rugby and association football. He was a keen mountaineer and gave lectures of his experiences in the Alps and the Pyrenees.

Next to the extension is the Communal Cemetery; there are two British graves either side of the main grass path: Sergeant Major W Pearce of the Loyal North Lancs, who died on 11 August 1916; and Lieutenant L Griffin of the Glosters, who died on 18 August 1916 (quite likely in the same incident as Captain Rorie). Why they were buried there and not in the already-existing extension will likely remain one of life's little mysteries.

Return to Rue Lamark and turn right. After 250 metres you will see the sign for **Bazentin-le-Petit Military Cemetery (2) (GPS**

Bazentin-le-Petit Military Cemetery. (*Author*)

5542272/0482937), on the western side of the village. Note as you walk up the approach path the wartime wire pickets supporting the fence. The cemetery was started at the end of July 1916, was initially called Singer Circus Cemetery and was used as a front line cemetery until as late as May 1917. It contains 182 dead, fifteen of them unidentified. The graves of thirty-three Germans were removed in 1923, thus explaining the gaps in the rows. The main use of the cemetery dates from October 1916; there was a dressing station close by during the March Retreat of 1918.

Private William Giles, 6th Battalion Australian Imperial Force. (*Australian War Memorial*)

Most of the graves are identified; there are fifty-five Australians buried here. In row D. 23 is 5390 Private William Giles, 6th Bn AIF from Richmond, Victoria. A 22-year-old driver prior to enlistment on 4 March 1916, he embarked for overseas with the 17th Reinforcements from Melbourne on 4 April 1916 aboard HMAT *Euripides*. He was killed in action near Flers on 4 February 1917.

6256 Private William Daly of the 4th Bn AIF died in February 1917, aged only 17. His grave is in Row H. 3. William was the son of Patrick and Mary Daly and he came from Mullenganda, New South Wales. (It is worth noting that if he was indeed 17 when he was killed, there is every possibility that he was only 16 when he enlisted. Another member of the Dominions who was a very underage late war casualty, was the South African David Ross, who was just a few months over 14 when he was killed in March 1918 and had already been wounded the previous year during Third Ypres.)

The CO of the 1st Australian Field Ambulance wrote in answer to an enquiry:

Private William Giles headstone. (*Author*)

17-year-old Private William
Daly, 4th Battalion AIF.
(*Australian War Memorial*)

Private William Daly's headstone.
(*Author*)

6256 Private W. Daly, 4th Bn. A. I. F. was brought to an aid post of this ambulance on 28th February 1917, suffering from bomb wounds of both legs – the legs being severed below the knees. He was suffering greatly from shock and died soon after admission. The burial took place next day at Singer Circus Cemetery, Bazentin-le-Petit.

Re-join your vehicle and continue to head northwards out the village. After 175 metres, where the road bends sharply to the left on to the D73 at what seems a crossroads, you will see the **Memorial to the Nine Brave Men (3) (GPS 5542476/0482928)** at the southwest corner of the crossroads. Stop (carefully! This road can carry heavy traffic.) and visit the memorial, noting the plaque on the back. It commemorates nine casualties of the 82nd Field Company RE who were killed in late July

Memorial to the Nine Brave Men. (*Author*)

162

1916 whilst carrying out work in the area. The original memorial was made from bricks obtained from the nearby ruined village, although over time many of these have had to be replaced. Return to your vehicle; take the minor looking road directly opposite the memorial, which leads to High Wood.

This road, badly potholed in places, will bring you out at the north west corner of High Wood. After 300 metres you will see on your right, on top of a bank and in a small copse, the private memorial to **Captain Houston SH Wallace (4) (GPS 5542581/0483228)**. Park here, watching you are not blocking the road for particularly wide farm vehicles. Captain Houston Wallace Hamilton of the 10/Worcesters was killed near here in the attack on High Wood on 22 July 1916. The memorial, originally erected by his aunt, was restored and rededicated with great ceremony in the 90s. Captain Wallace is commemorated by the CWGC on the Thiepval Memorial.

Return to your vehicle and as you travel along this road out of Bazentin-le-Petit note that the fields on either side saw intensive fighting for High Wood from 14 July 1916 and was consequently a maze of trenches. On your left, where the 50th Division was formed up for the attack on 15 September 1916, there were, for example, Intermediate, Swansea, Eye and Hook trenches; whilst on the right were Mill Street, Brecon and Junction trenches.

At the end of the road, some 1.6 kilometres after you joined it, you will meet the D107 Martinpuich-Longueval road; the north west corner of High Wood is in front of you. Turning right, after 340 metres you will see the imposing **London Cemetery and Extension (5) (GPS 5542955/0484419)** on your right-hand side, with High Wood on your left. Stop and visit the cemetery, there is ample parking space outside the cemetery.

The direction of attack on the 50th Divisional front in the capture of Martinpuich 15 September 1916. Martinpuich can be seen on the left, High Wood, which was being attacked by the 47th (London) Division, on the right. (*Author's collection*)

Entrance to London Cemetery and Extension. (*Author*)

The original London Cemetery was started when forty-seven men of the 47th (1/2nd London) Division were buried in a large shell hole on 18 and 21 September 1916. Other burials were added later, mainly of officers and men of the Division who died on 15 September 1916; at the Armistice the cemetery contained 101 graves. The cemetery was then greatly enlarged when remains were brought in from the surrounding battlefields, but the original battlefield cemetery is preserved within the larger cemetery, now known as the London Cemetery and Extension.

The cemetery is the third largest CWGC cemetery in the Somme; there are 3,873 Great War burials, the vast majority, 3,114, of them unidentified. It was used again in 1946 by the Army Graves Service for the reburial of 165 Second World War casualties recovered 'locally' from burial grounds where permanent maintenance was not possible. These graves are in one central plot at the extreme end of the cemetery, behind the Cross of Sacrifice. The original London Cemetery was designed by Sir Herbert Baker; but the site was completely re-modelled after the Second World War by Austin Blomfield.

Re-join your vehicle and turn around (carefully – this can be a busy road) and proceed towards Martinpuich. Just past the limit of High Wood you will be crossing the location of Eye Trench. Just as you enter the limits of Martinpuich you will see on your left a familiar green CWGC sign indicating **Martinpuich Communal and Military Cemeteries (6) (GPS5543950/0483000)** – note that it is a very sharp

Martinpuich Military Cemetery. (Author)

turn. These cemeteries are well worth a visit – see their entry in Walk 2 for details. The Military Cemetery is very close to the site of the German strongpoint Tangle South; there are good views to the west from the top of the cemetery.

Continue into the village and to the crossroads, where you might be startled by the sight of a life sized model cow. Turn right and drive 300 metres to Martinpuich Church (on your right) and the **47th Division Memorial complex (7) (GPS 5544192/0483127)**. Park by the church.

Aware that the passage of time since the end of the war had seen the decay of two temporary commemorative crosses erected at High

A postcard of Martinpuich Church. Although damaged by shelling, in the Battle of the Somme it was completely destroyed. (*Author*)

The 47th Division's Memorial gateway and boundary wall, leading to the memorial loggia; with the Martinpuich village war memorial framed by the gateway. (*Author*)

Wood and Eaucourt l'Abbaye, there was a serious worry that there would be nothing left in France to commemorate the record of the 47th (1/2nd London) Division or to associate the area with the 15,567 men who fell during the war whilst serving in its various units. Anxious that any memorial should be of real use to the community, the impressive – indeed unique – memorial complex comprising an entry arch, boundary wall, a large brick loggia and, not least, a playground, was dedicated on 25 September 1925. That date was significant, for in 1915 the Battle of Loos opened on that day and the Division formed the right flank of the attack – gaining its objectives on that first day. This was the 47th's first major action since it had arrived in France in March 1915 (although it was engaged in the Battle of Festubert). Thus, although the site selected reflects the extremely hard-fought actions in the area in which it was engaged and represents the brave actions of the 47th (London) Division around the village and especially the attack on High Wood on 15 September 1916, it serves to commemorate the work of the Division throughout the war.

The appeal for funds commenced on 29 November 1924; by 16 March the following year enough money had been raised to erect a permanent cross at High Wood and the arch, loggia and playground in Martinpuich. The accompanying children's playground even had a paddling pool and a sand pit!

Return to the village crossroads and turn right, signposted Le Sars. After a kilometre or so you will approach the Albert-Bapaume road, the D929. There is a safe place to park, off the main road, just before the junction and then walk carefully along the verge, paying attention to the fast moving traffic – there is now a (relatively) safe crossing place opposite it – to the **Canadian Somme Memorial (8) (GPS5544640/0482238)**

This memorial is situated on the D929, on the north (right side if heading

The Canadian Somme Memorial close to Courcelette. (*Author*)

towards Albert). The memorial is well maintained with no problems regarding access and this is also a fine opportunity to sit down on one of the benches and take time to reflect about the horrendous action here over a hundred years ago. This is also a perfect opportunity to have a snack and a drink. The memorial commemorates the part played in this area by the Canadians in the autumn of 1916, during which the 2nd Canadian Division took the village of Courcelette (and also attacked over the ground on the other side of the road, flanked by the 15th Division) in September 1916. Two months later their 4th Division comrades took the infamous Regina Trench. This lengthy trench, which under various names ran from St Pierre Divion on the Ancre to north east of Courcelette, was well placed and well constructed, protected by miles of thick barbed wire.

Re-join your vehicle and continue to the crossroads; turn right onto the D929 'Post Road' and continue towards Le Sars. On your left, after 1.8 kilometres, and shortly before the entrance to the village, you will pass the modern-day farm (Ferme du Château) that occupies the prewar site of Destremont Farm, which fell to the British on 29 September 1916. Drive slowly past this farm; within seconds, you will be driving across the location of the Flers 1 and 2 trenches. Enter Le Sars; you will soon come to the **Le Sars village crossroads (9) (GPS 5546520/0484350)**. On the right you will note an unusual, corrugated exterior gable wall on a well-maintained house situated immediately after the Mairie.

At the crossroads, turn right on to the D11, following the sign Gueudecourt – l'Abbaye d'Eaucourt and park as soon as you safely can, taking care that the vehicle does not block the road. Walk back to the crossroads. This point was pivotal in the taking of the village of Le Sars on 7 October. Standing facing the main road, the attack of the

The crossroads at Le Sars; note the house with the most unusual corrugated iron gabled end. (*Author*)

23rd Division on that day came from two general directions: on the left coming from your left to right along the main road through the village; and from the same general direction, but coming into the village from the area behind where you are standing. A machine gun positioned at the crossroads accounted for some seventy to eighty fleeing Germans.

Return to your vehicle and continue towards L'Abbaye d'Eaucourt, 1.3 kilometres away. Driving slowly along this road you will come

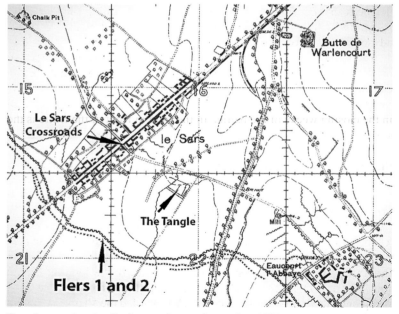

Trench map showing Le Sars and area, September 1916.

The Butte de Warlencourt, viewed from the Le Sars to l'Abbaye d'Eaucourt road. (*Author*)

across the location of some of the memorable sites of the battles in this area. After approximately 400 metres, on the right and some hundred metres or so in the field, is the site of the Maze trenches, part of the defences that confronted the right flank of the 23rd Division's attack. As you will have read in the battle narrative, several bodies of troops advanced up this road to the crossroads.

You will see the Butte de Warlencourt rising defiantly in the distance on the left after another 400 metres. The incline in front of the Butte can be clearly seen; the top of this incline was the location of The Nose, Snag Trench and The Tail, all features that involved very heavy fighting in the closing weeks of the battle. In the field in front of the Butte is the site of The Pimple and its various associated trenches. After another 200 metres or so, on your right and just a few metres into the field, is the site of Eaucourt l'Abbaye Mill, which fell to the 1/6th Londons on 5 October 1916.

Very shortly after this, at the very obvious left hand bend, you will have arrived at today's **L'Abbaye d'Eaucourt (10) (GPS 554570/485421)**. (At this point in the tour you will have travelled approximately eleven kilometres.) Park your vehicle here in front of the farm gates and take two minutes to enjoy the general vista of the battlefield from Le Sars to the Butte. There will be plenty of room to park. In the fighting here at Eaucourt on 1 October 1916 Roland Boys Bradford won the VC, Roland being one of two brothers (uniquely) to be awarded the Victoria Cross in the First World War.

L'Abbaye d'Eaucourt (Eaucourt l'Abbaye) viewed from the east. (*Author*)

Re-join your vehicle and head downhill away from L'Abbaye d'Eaucourt. After 250 metres, do NOT follow the road around the sharp bend to the right but go straight ahead, onto a minor **road to Le Barque (11) (GPS 5546050/0485668)**. (Note that the track on the left, at what was once a rural crossroads, comes out close to the Butte.) Stop at the first safe opportunity. You are now standing on, or very close to, the proposed starting point of two tanks in an attack on the Butte de Warlencourt of 28 October 1916. It did not take place due to the appalling weather conditions.

One tank was to proceed in the general direction of the road, ie in a north easterly direction, its objective being the German trench called Hook Sap, on the left-hand side of this road. The route of the other tank was to be in the direction of the Butte de Warlencourt and the Quarry situated beside it. The tank was to protect the right-hand side of the attack of the 50th Division. When the attack did eventually take place a week later the tanks were to take no part; no doubt the weather and conditions played a major part in this decision.

Return to your vehicle; after some 800 metres you will come to an upright rusty girder on the edge of the road beside you; stop. This is close to the site of **Hook Sap (12) (GPS5546528/0486251)**, which is situated some 300 metres to your left. This German strongpoint formed one side of a salient protruding into No Man's Land and formed part of the Gird Lines and Blind Trench system that covered the attack made by the 50th Division on 14 November.

Continue along this very quiet road to the main village crossroads in Le Barque-Thilloy, about two kilometres away. Drive slowly taking in the surrounding country. You will soon enter Ligny-Le Barque, which in due course will become Ligny-Thilloy and then Thilloy. Keep following the Rue d'Abbaye; at the cross roads, with a bus stop on your left, turn right onto the D10E1, here called Rue de Miraumont. After 750 metres you will see the church on the left of the road; opposite is the Mairie.

Information board about Major L E G Hawker VC DSO. (*Author*)

Park your vehicle and visit the **Major Lanoe Hawker VC DSO Memorial (13) (GPS 5548040/0487700)** in front of the church. Note there are a few steps leading to the monument. On 23 November, just after the Battle of the Somme ended, Hawker took part in an air patrol near Bapaume. After attacking numerous German aircraft over Achiet, Hawker began a long dog-fight with one in particular. The pilot was the German 'ace' Manfred von Richthofen, who later wrote, *I discovered that I was not meeting a beginner. He had not the slightest intention of breaking off the fight...* The battle lasted for more than thirty minutes until, Hawker running out of fuel, he was finally brought down and killed, von Richthofen's eleventh victim. He was dead when his plane crashed into a field on the west side of the road from Factory Corner to Ligny Thilloy, at a point roughly midway between the two places. Hawker was aged just 25 when he died. Although he was known to have been buried at the time (indeed there are photographs of his grave marker), his remains were lost in later fighting and he is now commemorated on the Arras Flying Services Memorial.

By September 1916 the Germans' air capability was rapidly improving. The building up of previously weak air reconnaissance and bomber groups, combined with improved aircraft, had enabled the Germans to become far more effective in the sky. The formation of *Jagdstaffeln* (fighter – literally hunting – units) made it possible by mid-September for the Germans to challenge the air superiority of the Allies

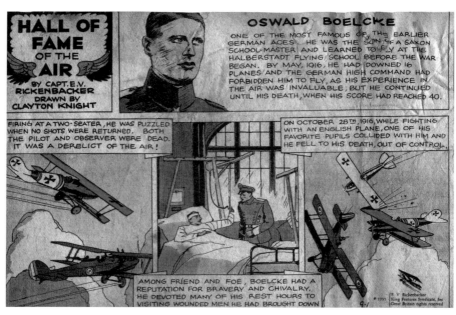

Oswald Boelcke – *Hall of Fame of the Air*. (*Author*)

over the Somme; here the twelve warplanes, single seater fighters, of Hauptmann Oswald Boelcke's Jasta 2 won almost legendary fame. Boelcke alone shot down forty enemy aircraft, twenty of them over the Somme. He was decorated with the Pour le Mérite. He was killed as the result of a collision with a colleague's plane on 28 October 1916 here at Ligny Thilloy.

Go back to your vehicle and continue along the D10E1; after 275 metres you will come to the D10 Bapaume-Flers road. Turn right and after 300 metres you come to **Ligny-Thilloy Communal Cemetery (14) (5547587/0487903)** on your left.

The memorial to the 1870–1871 war in Ligny Thilloy cemetery. (*Author*)

Park on the track on the left of the cemetery and enter through the top left gate (when standing facing the cemetery from the road). There is a memorial cenotaph in front of the large cross to the 1870–1871 Franco Prussian War and those killed at Ligny-Thilloy on 2–3 January 1871; it also commemorates those killed in the Great War and who are buried in the cemetery.

Return to your vehicle, turn around and turn right, retracing your route and continuing on the D10 for some three kilometres until you arrive in the southern outskirts of Bapaume and the junction with the D917 Bapaume-Péronne road. The Hôtel de la Paix is on your left. Beware the police station near the outskirts of the town here; many an unsuspecting motorist has been caught there by the dreaded speed gun. You are about to visit **Bapaume Australian Cemetery (15) (GPS 5549934/0489589)**, which is signposted and is situated at the back of the houses facing you at the junction. With great care, as the traffic is heavy here, head across the junction, onto Rue du Chemin Blanc, which inclines sharply to the left, and which then sweeps to the right behind houses. After approximately 150 metres you will reach the cemetery, on your right.

Major William Macauley's headstone, Bapaume Australian Cemetery. (*Author*)

The German head stones in Bapaume Australian Cemetery. (*Author*)

The cemetery was begun in the spring of 1917 by the 3rd Australian Casualty Clearing station and was only in use for a few months; however, it was used when the Germans were in occupation in April and May 1918, which explains the German graves in Row C (ie on your left as you enter). There was a much larger German cemetery nearby, with over 160 burials. These were concentrated into Villers-au-Flos German Cemetery, which is about six kilometres to the south east from here and holds a little under 2,500 burials: a number of the wartime German cemeteries in the area covered by this book were very likely concentrated there post war.

One unusual casualty in the cemetery is Major William Ingham Macauley, Royal Army Veterinary Corps, who died on 14 May 1917 (B.33). There are relatively few Veterinary Corps graves, given the significant numbers required to look after the hundreds of thousands of horses and mules used by the BEF. He was a member of the supervising staff – probably at Corps, possibly at divisional, level – when his body was found in the front line with a single gunshot wound, which was said to be self-inflicted. He was mentioned in despatches twice.

Return to the D917 Bapaume-Péronne road and turn right, heading into Bapaume. Be warned that there are some rather disconcertingly 'vigorous' 'sleeping policemen' arrangements in the town, particularly as you come into the central area. In due course you will see the imposing statue to commemorate **General Louis Faidherbe (16) (GPS**

The statue of General Louis Faidherbe stands proudly in the centre of Bapaume. The base of the statue clearly shows the signs of war. (*Author*)

233. BAPAUME — Monument et place Faidherbe
Monument and Square Faidherbe

The Faidherbe memorial's base after the war. (*Author*)

5550166/0489243), which stands in front of the Hôtel de Ville. Park as best you can and view the monument.

If required, the tourist information office is on the left behind the monument, just past the Hôtel de Ville. Now perhaps is a good time to have a coffee or a meal. Bapaume has a compact centre, and there are a number of eateries and cafés. There are supermarkets on the outskirts, particularly to the south and north; and one close to the route taken when we leave Bapaume on this tour (turn left towards Albert and it is almost immediately on your right). Be wary of the lunch break, from 12.00 pm until 2.00 pm, which is frequently adhered to in this region of France. Perhaps surprisingly, this sometimes applies to cafés!

Bapaume, which was adopted by Sheffield after the war, was a fortified town (remnants of the town walls still exist) and has had a colourful history over the centuries. During (and before) the Somme 1916 it was the site of a German Corps headquarters and was a major support and administrative area – a sort of German Albert but further in the rear, at least until the Offensive began.

The Germans made full use of the many cellars, some quite extensive, that lie beneath the streets and houses. Cellar entrances can be seen at times; one major entrance is only thirty metres in front of the statue of Faidherbe. On the corner of the Rue d'Arras are double covers in the pavement that are normally opened to the public in September.

175

When the Germans evacuated Bapaume in March 1917 they left many of the buildings booby-trapped or mined. The Hôtel de Ville was one such building. This mine was operated by a delayed, chemical fuse, set more than eight days previously. A steel wire was suspended in acid; when the acid ate through it this released a spring, in turn operating the striker and thus firing the mine. It had been left as a trap, in the hope that a division would place its headquarters there. No senior staff had occupied the building when it exploded; but about thirty men, including those employed at the coffee stall of the Australian Comforts Fund, and two visiting French parliamentary deputies, Captain R. Briquet and Albert Tallandier, were sleeping there when the explosion took place. The two deputies and the Comforts Fund men were killed but rescue work throughout that night and the next day meant that six others were brought out alive. The Germans re-entered the ruins of Bapaume on 24 March 1918 but were ejected by the New Zealand Division late the following August. After the war the town was awarded the Croix de Guerre and the Légion d'Honneur.

The 1870–1871 war arrives in the vicinity of Bapaume.

France, like many countries, is not good at remembering national defeats, not least the capitulation at Sedan and the capture of her emperor in September 1870. Instead there is a tendency to make much of limited victories. One such example is the Battle of Bapaume (3 January 1871), which the French viewed as a startling, almost miraculous, victory achieved by the Army of the North under General Faidherbe. This French success became a symbol of Bapaume, the town's victory bells ringing in the ears of the population and restoring some national pride. To others less involved, the result of the battle was a draw, resulting in the opposing armies mutually withdrawing from the battlefield.

On 19 July 1870 France declared war on Prussia, at the time one of the many (albeit the most powerful) states that together constituted Germany, at the time a geographical term rather than a political one. Its origins are too complex to discuss here. The first battles of the war took place in Alsace, on the Franco-German border, within a week of its declaration, on 2 July. The 1870–71 War, known to the French as simply 'In 70', was remarkably short. In less than two months Napoleon III and his army capitulated at Sedan and a republic was proclaimed in Paris. By the end of January 1871 the French armies were defeated and an armistice was signed on 28 January 1871 when besieged Paris fell. The peace treaty of May

1871 saw France lose the bulk of the départements of Alsace and Lorraine to the newly created German Empire.

The French army was substantially reorganised following the war, these reforms starting within a year of its ending. Between 1872 and 1905 a series of laws were passed that created mandatory full-time service for all citizens (which, inevitably, did not mean that in reality: although a fairly high proportion of young men were, indeed, conscripted). National defence was high on the political agenda but 'revenge' on the Germans for the insult of 1870–71 was not to happen for almost another fifty years.

After the twin disasters of Sedan and Metz (although the besieged army in the latter did not surrender until 27 October, in reality its fate was sealed weeks earlier), the French Armée du Nord was built on the 22ème Corps, headquartered at Lille and commanded by General Bourbaki. On 18 November 1870 the Armée du Nord was created on the orders of the new republican government in Paris, under the command of General Farre. Soon afterwards, on 3 December, he was replaced by General Louis Faidherbe, born in Lille on 3 June 1818. The 22ème Corps had three very understrength and scattered divisions: the first commanded by General Lecointe, the second by General Paulze d'Ivoy and the third by Amiral Houlac. By mid December a second corps, the 23ème, had been created.

The war arrived in the Picardy area in November 1870 when several actions took place between General Edwin von Manteuffel's First Army and the Armée du Nord under Bourbaki and Faidherbe. There were actions near Amiens on 27 November 1870 (including what became known as the Battle of Villers-Bretonneux) and at Pont Noyelles (or Hallue) on 23–24 December 1870. Faidherbe was one of the few French commanders to emerge from the war with any sort of respectable reputation, based on the French performance at the indecisive Battle of Pont Noyelles/Hallue, followed by partial success at the Battle of Bapaume on 2–3 January 1871.

General Louis Faidherbe.
(*Wikimedia Commons*)

The Bapaume area was occupied by the Prussians towards the end of December 1870, provoking General Faidherbe's Armée du Nord to commence operations to lift the Prussian siege of Péronne, a fortified town and a key crossing point of the Somme, some twenty-two kilometres south of Bapaume. The war was difficult to support for the local population: the two armies had a poor supply system and consequently Bapaume and the surrounding villages suffered from requisitioning and pillaging as a daily event. Nobody was spared; on top of this (as was perfectly usual practice in the warfare of the time and was to be repeated in 1914) the communes of Bapaume and Bertincourt (several kilometres east of Bapaume) were forced to pay levies, in their cases coming to a combined total of more than 1,500,000 francs.

Péronne came under siege from 27 December 1870, the bombardment commenced on 28 December and the town surrendered on 10 January 1871; the Germans appreciated the military usefulness of the nearby high ground of Mont St Quentin (to the north) and La Maisonette (to the south west). Both heights gained considerable notoriety in the First World War. Faidherbe, who had withdrawn

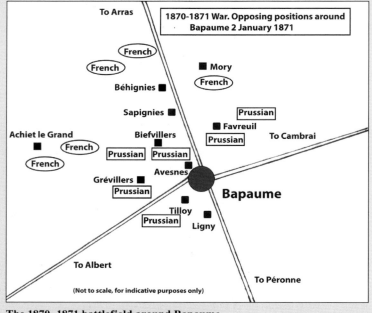

The 1870–1871 battlefield around Bapaume.

to a line between Arras and Douai and was rebuilding his Army, determined to intervene and lift the siege.

The Battle of Bapaume (involving about 15,000 men on the German/Prussian side and 25,000 on the French) took place in several of the communes surrounding the town, notably Béhagnies and Biefvillers-lès-Bapaume. Despite a neutral result – although in reality the French failed in their objective of raising the siege of Péronne – the outcome did mean that the Pas de Calais was not invaded by the Prussian army.

The battle started on 2 January 1871, a bitter, ice-cold day. In January that year the temperature was to fall to nearly -18 degrees centigrade. Towards midday the opposing armies met at nearby Béhagnies, about five kilometres from Bapaume, and a brisk engagement followed. The French attack failed; however, the Prussians abandoned the village during the night of 3–4 January, concerned about the French presence in the nearby village of Bihucourt.

The village of Biefvillers-lès-Bapaume lay on the march of generals du Bessol and Faidherbe, a route which led from Achiet le Grand to Bapaume, seven kilometres away. A Prussian division was based in Biefvillers-lès-Bapaume, which had a defensive line that ran from Grévillers to Beugnatre. In the morning of 3 January fighting broke out in the village; hand to hand fighting with bayonets saw the village captured, house by house, from the Prussians. The bulk of the German soldiers in the 33e R.I. were Prussians from that part of Poland annexed a century or more earlier. The French pursued the Prussians to the edge of Bapaume, where skirmishes took place between French snipers and the Prussian Uhlans (cavalry). Despite seeming to be in a position of strength, for various reasons Faidherbe ordered a withdrawal to the north. The Prussians, similarly, left Bapaume and fell back on Péronne, which capitulated on 9 January 1871. The two-day battle was over. Bapaume had been spared. On the French side, the battle of Bapaume resulted in 1319 dead and 800 men missing or deserted (other figures suggest about 1,600 dead); The German suffered about 800 dead, although some suggest a figure nearer 1100.

The war of 1870–71 left a profound mark on the French. Many memorials were erected on the battlefields, encouraged by the local committees of a private organization, Souvenir Français, founded in 1887. Successive governments highlighted the graves of the fallen soldiers; simple stone headstones and monuments – columns, obelisks and pyramids, provided the focus of commemorations. In Bapaume, streets in the town still carry the name of the generals of the Armée du Nord: eg Lecointe, Derroja and (naval) Captain Payen.

Today, in front of the Hôtel de Ville of Bapaume, stands the statue of General Faidherbe (who died in 1889), the work of local sculptor Louis Noel, who was born in St Omer. Unveiled on 29 September 1890, the anniversary of Faidherbe's death, the statue was pulled down by the Germans during their occupation, possibly thinking it was made of bronze, possibly because he represented French resistance. It disappeared shortly thereafter. Its base, scarred by the marks of the war, remained vacant for thirteen years. In 1926 the commune commissioned Jules Déchin, the stepson of the original sculptor, to create a new statue, working from the original plans. The replacement was unveiled on 18 August 1929 by Paul Painlevé, the French Minister of War. As part of the refurbishment of the square in Bapaume in September 1997, the statue and its original base were moved to a new position in front of the Hôtel de Ville. During the move a lead plaque was discovered below the base, which included the names of the town's municipal councillors of over a century earlier, when the statue was first erected.

The 1870–1871 War Memorial in Bapaume Communal Cemetery today. (Author)

There are several memorials in the area that commemorate the war of 1870–71. In the communal cemetery, situated on the outskirts of Bapaume, at the north end of Rue Faubourg d'Arras, is the site of a large cross memorial and the burial place of 186 of the combatants. It was blessed in 3 January 1872, a year after the battle ended. In nearby Favreuil lie twenty-eight French and nine German soldiers; whilst in Biefvillers-lès-Bapaume there are 290 French and German casualties. In Béhagnies, the ossuary holds sixty-seven French and three Prussian soldiers. In Ligny-Thilloy there is a memorial in the local cemetery just outside the south of the village, on the road to Flers. Probably the most visited and pictured memorial is situated a kilometre or so north of the first roundabout (part of the ring road) leaving Bapaume on the main road to Arras. Formed of the large numbers 1870–1871, it is on the south west side of the crossroads to Bapaume, Biefvillers-lès-Bapaume, Favreuil and Arras. The monument was erected by the Conseil Général du Pas de Calais after effective petitioning by the 'Bapaumois', who wished to see a memorial in the location. Behind the monument is the grave of a Prussian soldier. Interestingly, the peace treaty allowed for the erection of Prussian/German memorials and burials in France; whilst there were – and, to a large extent, still are – a surprising number of these still in the Metz-Sedan region, they are, effectively, non-existent in this area.

The 1870–1871 Memorial at about the time of the Great War. (Author)

Leave Bapaume by Rue Faubourg d'Arras, the road leading to the left if you are facing the Faidherbe. [Note: After 500 metres or so, there is a turning to Albert – if you go down there, almost immediately you will come to a supermarket and a self service petrol station on your right.] After 800 metres, approaching the northern outskirts of the town, stop at **Bapaume Communal Cemetery (17) (GPS 5551083/0489048)**, on your right (there is parking outside it). There are allied graves in groups scattered throughout the cemetery. Of the twenty-five CWGC burials, most are Australians from the early days of the capture of Bapaume at the end of March 1917; there are some New Zealanders from August 1918 and one casualty from September 1944. There is a somewhat weather-beaten memorial to General Faidherbe and the ossuary discussed above.

Amongst the members of the AIF buried here is Second Lieutenant Herbert William Brough, Australian Field Artillery (his original marker says he was a member of the 105th Howitzer Battery), who died on 1 May 1917. Brough, who was born in Sydney, was the son of the Reverend Anthony Watson Brough and Rosetta Jane Brough, of The London Mission, Erode, South India.

The original grave marker of Herbert Brough. (*Australian War Memorial*)

Second Lieutenant Herbert Brough's headstone. (*Author*)

The eye-catching 1870–1871 memorial on the D917 Bapaume to Arras Road. (*Author*)

Continue north and follow the road to Arras (D917) at the next roundabout. After 800 metres you come to a crossroads; the large **memorial to the 1870–1871 Battle of Bapaume (18) (GPS 5552232/0488915)** is on your left. Turn right, direction Favreuil (D10E3), and stop as soon as is practicable to get a good view of this imposing 1870–1871 memorial (note that the D917 is a busy road).

The **Communal Cemetery in Favreuil (19) (GPS 5552711/0490140)** is located 300 metres east of the church and can be easily missed. On entering Favreuil, turn left at the village crossroads onto the D36E4; drive past the mairie and the splendid 'blue' war memorial, which is situated on your right. 250 metres after the memorial, turn right onto Rue de Cimetière and proceed for 500 metres, crossing over the Rue de l'Église. The 1870–71 memorial, particularly commemorating the fallen of 3 January 1871, is at the very top of the cemetery. You will notice a small circular red and white 'button', with a motif in blue: this is the badge of Souvenir Français and is found on numerous war memorials and often isolated war related graves in France and of which they take an especial care.

The 1870–1871 War Memorial in Favreuil Cemetery, where twenty-eight French and nine German soldiers lie. (*Author*)

The splendid Favreuil War Memorial. (*Author*)

Favreuil British Cemetery. (*Author*)

Retrace your route to the main street and turn left at the junction. Pass the mairie and at the next junction turn left onto the D10E3; on your right, after approximately 700 metres and up an approach path, is **Favreuil British Cemetery (20) (GPS 5552394/0490171)**. It was used by the British from April 1917 to March 1918 and in the later months of the war in 1918.

After the war its size was increased by the concentration of graves from local smaller and isolated burial grounds. The village was retaken in August 1918 by the 37th and New Zealand Divisions. The German cemetery, which lay adjacent to the north west, and which contained 484 graves, was removed. A British soldier in it could not be identified when the

The final resting place of Serjeant Harold Evans DCM MM. (*Author*)

cemetery was removed, so a special memorial to the soldier was erected in the British cemetery. Among the 387 British graves is Serjeant Harold Evans DCM MM (Plot II C.5.), 2nd West Yorkshire (Prince of Wales's Own), who was killed in action on 20 November 1917, the opening day of the Battle of Cambrai. He was awarded his DCM for his qualities of leadership. The VC was the only military decoration for valour that could be awarded for an action (a rule that remained in force until relatively recently) that resulted in the recipient's death, ie posthumously. Evans' DCM was gazetted in April 1918, long after he was killed, but related to actions that took place before the one in which he was killed. There is a row of German headstones along the right side of the cemetery.

Return to your vehicle and retrace your route through Favreuil to the 1870–1871 memorial on the D917 Arras road. Turn right and after 1.5 kilometres you will reach Sapignies. On the left there is a signpost for the rarely visited **Sapignies German Cemetery (21) (GPS 5553422/0488087)** and for *Centre*. Turn left on to the D31E1, Rue Principale, which leads to the cemetery. You will come to the church after 300 metres and the cemetery is some seventy-five metres down a road opposite the church. The cemetery stands above the level of the road; beware the steep stairs up to the main gate.

Compare the austerity of this cemetery to those British ones that you have already visited. This difference was in part a consequence of a clause of the Treaty of Versailles relating to German war dead and German memorials. The cemetery was used until March 1917, primarily during the period of the 1916 Battle of the Somme. It was used again in 1918 when the Germans returned to the area, from spring 1918 until August 1918. In 1924 more than 400 German soldiers were relocated here from local civil cemeteries and burial grounds between Favreuil and Sapignies; and in 1927–28 it was put in order and the horticulture established. In 1977 the markers were replaced with their current metal ones.

Sapignies German Cemetery. (*Author*)

Return to the Arras road, the D917; as you leave the cemetery, note the village war memorial that is (unusually) attached to the wall of the church, left of the entrance porch.

Turn left on the D917. After about 700 metres, in Béhagnies turn left on to Rue de Bapaume, which takes you into the centre of the village; after 300 metres, follow the road leading to the left (the D31) and after a few metres the church is on the right. Park. **Béhagnies Church Battle of Bapaume Monument (22) (GPS 5554337/0487850)** is in front of the church (it doubles as a memorial to later wars), under which, unusually, sixty-seven French and three Prussian soldiers are buried.

Béhagnies 1870–1871 Memorial. (*Author*)

Continue on the D31 for nearly 3.5 kilometres, which will take you through Bihucourt to a junction with the D7 Bapaume road. Turn right and drive into Achiet-le-Grand. At the roundabout, just after the church of St Jean Baptiste and St Brice on

Achiet-le-Grand Communal Cemetery Extension. (*Author*)

186

One of three brothers to die in the First World War, Bombardier E. Watmough of the Royal Field Artillery. (*Author*)

Executed for desertion, Private Arthur Mitchell. Notice that his is amongst a number of headstones in the cemetery that have been recently completely replaced, part of the continuing maintenance work of the CWGC. (*Author*)

The headstone of Second Lieutenant George Doughty RFC. Note that the cap badge is incorrect: it should be that of the Royal Flying Corps. (*Author*)

Second Lieutenant Ian Cameron RFC. (*Author*)

your left, go straight on, straight over the following crossroads and join the D74e, which leads on to the D32, running parallel with the railway lines northward out of the village. After 800 metres the road sweeps to the left under the railway lines. Straight afterwards turn sharp left on to Rue de la Laitierie. **Achiet-le-Grand Communal Cemetery Extension (23) (GPS 5553769/0483954)** is up the second street on the right –Rue de l'Égalite.

Opened in the spring of 1917, the cemetery was used by the 45th and 49th Casualty Clearing Stations (located here, amongst other reasons, because of the proximity of the railway line) until March 1918. The Germans used the cemetery briefly in 1918 before it returned to British hands in August 1918. The extension was expanded by the addition of nearly 650 graves after the war and it now has 1259 identified casualties.

Buried here is a deserter who was executed on 20 August 1917. Private Arthur Mitchell (Plot IV R. 3) of the 1st/6th Lancashire Fusiliers served in Gallipoli and went absent after spending six months on the Western Front. He was arrested nine days later behind the lines, working in the fields and wearing blue trousers and (as you do) a policeman's 'bonnet'. One of three brothers to die in the war is buried here. Bombardier E Watmough (III. K. 3.) of the Royal Field Artillery died on 31 August 1918, aged 27. His brother John died on 10 July 1915 and is buried in Ridge Wood Military Cemetery in Belgium and the third brother, Victor, died at the age of 19 and is commemorated on the Tyne Cot Memorial. The cemetery has an unusually large number (thirty-six) of BEF aviators buried there. Amongst them are Second Lieutenants Ian Cameron (II M. 19) and George Doughty (II.M.6), who were the eighth and tenth victims of the Red Baron, both shot down in November 1916.

Leave the cemetery and retrace your route, following the railway lines and passing the Hôtel de la Gare into the centre of Achiet le Grand. At the crossroads go straight on and follow the D7, heading towards Biefvillers-lès-Bapaume. After 3.5 kilometres, at a seemingly random traffic light, Biefvillers-

Biefvillers-lès-Bapaume 1870–1871 War Memorial. (*Author*)

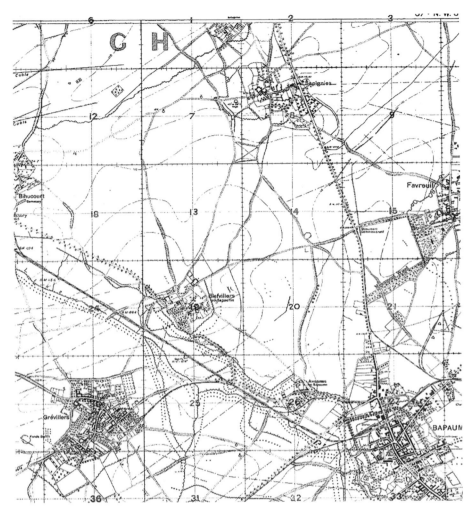

A trench map dated 27 November 1916 showing the extensive German defence network around Grévillers, Sapignies and Favreuil area.

lès-Bapaume is signposted to the left. Turn left on to the D103E and after about fifty metres, stop. The village's **War Memorial (24) (GPS 5551540/0487140)** is on your left. Once more it also commemorates the fallen of the Franco-Prussian War. The memorial is one of those erected by Souvenir Français (in October 1894); it is unusual in that not only does it commemorate individuals but also regiments that participated in the Battle of Bapaume.

The imposing entrance to Grévillers Military Cemetery. (*Author*)

Return to the D7 and turn left. After 1.2 kilometres, you will reach a roundabout; take the first right, signposted Grévillers, on to the D29; after 700 metres, just short of the entrance to the village and on your right, is **Grévillers Military Cemetery (25) (GPS 5550623/0487118)**. Stop and visit this very pleasant, well maintained cemetery.

The village of Grévillers was occupied by the BEF on 14 March 1917. In April and May, the 3rd, 29th and 3rd Australian Casualty Clearing Stations were located nearby. They used the cemetery until March 1918, when Grévillers was lost to the Germans during their great advance. On the following 24 August, the New Zealand Division recaptured it and in September various Casualty Clearing Stations came to the village and used the cemetery again. After the Armistice, 200 graves were brought in from the battlefields to the south of the village. There are now 2,106 British and Dominion servicemen of the Great War buried or commemorated here. 189 of the burials are unidentified; but there are special memorials to eighteen casualties known or believed to be buried among them. Other special memorials record the names of two casualties buried in Avesnes-lès-Bapaume German Cemetery whose graves could not be found. The cemetery also contains the graves of seven Second World War airmen, and eighteen French graves. Most of the Second World War graves are casualties of a Lancaster bomber shot

Private Miller Mafaking Fergusson.
(*Australian War Memorial*)

down on 14 July 1943 following a raid on Aachen. The French graves are situated near the Cross of Sacrifice.

At the rear of the cemetery is the Grévillers (New Zealand) Memorial, which commemorates almost 450 officers and men of the New Zealand Division who died in fighting in the area from March to August 1918, and in the Allied advance between 8 August and 11 November 1918, and who have no known grave. This is one of seven New Zealand memorials in France and Belgium to those of her soldiers who died on the Western Front and whose graves are not known. The memorials are all in cemeteries chosen as appropriate to

Particulars Required for the Roll of Honour of Australia in the Memorial War Museum.

NOTED ON H.R. CARD

1. Name (in full) of Fallen Soldier *Miller Mafaking Fergusson*
2. Unit and Number (if known) *27 Battalion. No. 76082 Private*
3. With what Town or District in Australia was he chiefly connected (under which his name ought to come on the Memorial)—
   Town (if any) *Moonta* District *Wakefield* State *South Australia*
4. What was his Birthplace *Quorn*
5. Date of Death *May 5th 1917*
6. Place where Killed or Wounded *Bullecourt*

Particulars Required for the Nation's Histories.

1. What was his Calling *In Field Gun Section.*
2. Age at time of Death *16 years and four months.*
3. What was his School *Public School.*
4. What was his other Training
5. If born in Britain or Abroad, at what age did he come to Australia
6. Had he ever served in any Military or Naval Force before Enlisting in the A.I.F. (Please state particulars) *H.C. was a cadet*
7. Any other biographical details likely to be of interest to the Historian of the A.I.F., or of his Regiment—

8. Was he connected with any other Member of the A.I.F. who died or who distinguished himself. (Please state Relationship) *He had a cousin killed in action. also 5 cousins and two brothers taking part in the war.*
9. Name and Address of the Parent or other person giving this information—
   Name *A. Fergusson*
   Relationship to Soldier *Mother*
   Address *Quorn South Australia*
10. Names and Addresses of any other persons to whom reference could be made by the Historian for further information—
   Name
   Address

NOTE.—This Folder is Addressed to the Secretary, Department of Defence, Melbourne. Please fold in four, and stick down gummed flap so that the addressed portion is outside. The information is required urgently.

1885/10.11.—C.16706.

Details provided by his mother to the Australian War Memorial.

the fighting in which the men died. The cemetery and memorial were designed by Sir Edwin Lutyens.

Private Miller Mafaking [sic] Fergusson 27th Battalion AIF. was a labourer from Quorn, South Australia. His middle name almost certainly celebrated the relief of Mafeking during the Second Boer War. He joined the 27th Battalion on 9 April 1917, was wounded in action near Bapaume on 5 May 1917 and died later that day. Private Fergusson is buried in Plot III D. 8. His mother wrote that he was 16 years and 4 months when he died; and that he had two brothers who also served in the war. Forms were sent to next of kin seeking details regarding the deceased for the records of the Australian War Memorial in Canberra. The completed circular for Private Fergusson is shown.

The headstone of Private MM Fergusson AIF. (*Author*)

Continue into Grévillers. After 570 metres the main road turns sharply right; 180 metres further on, in the centre of the village and with the war memorial on your left, you will see a sign pointing left to Warlencourt. This can be easily missed as the road bends to the right at that point. Go left, following Grand Rue, which leads out of the village to the south. On leaving the village and on both sides of the road you will soon see, running parallel to the main road, the remains of a Second World War German airfield (although originally started by the BEF in 1940), with the runway being on your left. Much of the runway – indeed practically all of it, has been ploughed over; but

The private memorial to Lieutenant Commander Oswald Wainwright RN of Hawke Battalion, 63rd (Royal Naval) Division in Loupart Wood, near Warlencourt. (*Author*)

192

aircraft dispersal areas still exist and the whole thing stretched north up to the road to Miraumont.

After 1.5 kilometres a large wood, Loupart Wood, will be on your right. Follow the road for another 500 metres to the southern end of the wood, where you will see a house beside a track with a 20 kilometres per hour sign. Turn right off the road and head to the track leading to the wood. At the entrance to the wood it is suggested you park your vehicle and walk the short distance up the main path in the woods to the memorial to **Lieutenant Commander Oswald Wainwright (26) (GPS 5549624/0484907).** Wainwright was a company commander of Hawke Battalion, 63rd (Royal Naval) Division, who was killed here on 25 August 1918 whilst attempting to destroy a German machine-gun post. His body was never found. The memorial, erected with the support of the local commune, was unveiled in the summer of 2005.

Return to the main road, and turn right to Warlencourt. After 1.3 kilometres you come to a junction with the D10E1. There are great views from here of the Butte de Warlencourt, on the other side of the Albert-Bapaume road.

Turn right, heading into Warlencourt; you will soon pass the village war memorial on your right. Proceed through Warlencourt, over the crossroads, in the direction of Pys. After 1.3 kilometres, where the road bends (Pys can be seen in the distance at roughly 11 o'clock), you have reached the site of **German gun emplacements (27) GPS 5548390/0483832)** that can be seen on the original RFC photo. Note

The Butte de Warlencourt, viewed from the junction near Warlencourt village. The D929, the Bapaume road, runs across the centre of the photograph. (*Author*)

Original RFC aerial photograph of the German gun positions near Warlencourt on the Pys road. (*Author*)

Trench map dated 1 January 2017 showing the above location.

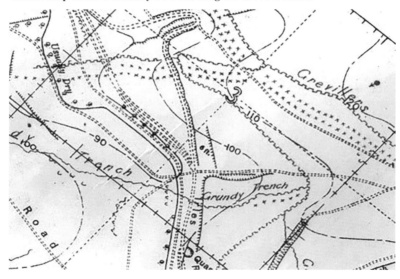

in the picture the large German trench, Coulee Trench, which ran in front of you and on to the top of the fields to your right, where it joined Grévillers Trench.

Follow this road for 1.3 kilometres towards Pys, turning left at the junction with the D74, which will bring you into Le Sars from the north

The quarry situated near Le Sars on the road from Pys. (*Author*)

east. After 1.3 kilometres you will see a wood on your right. This is what has become the rather large (and certainly not what its name suggests) Petit Bois Casimir; just beyond the end of the wood and on your left is the entrance to **Le Sars Quarry (28) (GPS 5547131/0483850)**. This was the quarry taken by the 23rd Division on 8 October and from which they then met up with their Canadian neighbours to their left. Stop and have a look around the Quarry but be careful underfoot. There is still some battlefield debris lying about: look, photograph, but do not touch!

Leave the quarry and continue along the D74 and within 900 metres you have reached the crossroads at Le Sars, where you were several hours ago if you have followed this tour in its entirety. At the crossroads turn left, go through Le Sars and, 600 metres from the outskirts of the village, you will see signposted, up a narrow road, the **Butte de Warlencourt (29) (GPS 5547086/0485310)**. Originating back to late Roman times, the Butte (French for mound) is a mound some sixty feet high, standing close to the D929 Albert-Bapaume road. Held by the Germans at the end of the Somme in 1916, it marked the final line of the British advance on the Somme in 1916 in this area, although it has been seen as having a wider significance, symbolising the limit of the advance of that offensive which was launched with such high hopes on 1 July. According to the British Official Historian, the Butte was:

'... a chalk mound some sixty feet high, on the slope of a spur overlooking the Bapaume road. The Butte afforded excellent observation of the low ground to the south west and to Bapaume in the opposite direction, in which area were many battery positions; its importance was fully appreciated by both the British and Germans.'

However, Charles Carrington, in his classic Great War memoir *Soldiers from the Wars Returning* exclaimed (perhaps more accurately):

'... the Butte of Warlencourt terrified us. A dome of gleaming white chalk from which all the vegetation had been blown away by shellfire, it was the most conspicuous object in the landscape by daylight or moonlight. The Butte seemed to tower over you and threaten you. We did three tours in this sector in November and December, the worst in my experience.'

Enter the well-maintained site and take the walkway to the top. The views are excellent. There are a number of very informative information boards on the site. The orientation board is very useful for showing your position in relation to other points of interest on the battlefield. If you have completed this vehicle tour you will have made a full 360-degree tour of the Butte area.

The visit to the Butte completes the tour and it is now time to withdraw to base for a coffee or something perhaps slightly stronger. You will have covered the battlegrounds in the area of Martinpuich, Le Sars, the Butte de Warlencourt and Bapaume and its surrounds, including areas fought over in 1917 and in 1918; of an area where the troops of Faidherbe's Armée du Nord fought against the Prussians some forty-five years previously, in January 1871; and even seen something of a Luftwaffe air base from the Second World War.

The Butte de Warlencourt seen from above today. (*Stevie Kerr*)

Selected Reading and Bibliography

English Language Sources

47th (London) Division War Memorials High Wood and Martinpuich: Committee of 47th (London) Division, 1925

A History of The Black Watch (Royal Highlanders) in the Great War, 1914–1919, Volume Three: New Army: Wauchope, Major-General, C.B., The Naval & Military Press

A Subaltern's Odyssey: Talbot Kelly, R.B., William Kimber & Co. Limited, 1980

Battleground Europe, Somme, Beaumont Hamel Newfoundland Park: Cave Nigel, Leo Cooper 2003

Before Endeavours Fade: Coombs, Rose E.B., After the Battle, (13th edition) 2006

Douglas Haig War Diaries and Letters 1914–1918: Sheffield, Gary and Bourne, John, BCA, 2005

Fighting the Somme: Sheldon, Jack, Pen and Sword, 2017

Germans on the Somme: Bilton, David, Pen and Sword, 2009

History of the Great War Based on Official Documents – Military Operations France and Belgium, 1916 2nd July 1916 to the end of the Battles of the Somme: Miles, Captain Wilfred, Macmillan & Co. Limited, 1938

Illustrative Michelin Guides to the Battlefields (1914–1918) The Somme Volume 1: Michelin & Cie, G.S. Smith, 1993

Kitchener's Army – The Raising of the New Armies 1914–1916: Simkins, Peter, Pen and Sword, 2007

Major& Mrs Holt's Battlefield guide to the Somme: Holt, Tonie & Valmai, Leo Cooper, 2003

Q. 6. A and Other Places: Recollections of 1916, 1917 and 1918: Buckley, Francis, Spottiswoode, Ballantyne & Co. Ltd, 1920 – Project Gutenberg eBook www.gutenberg.net, 2008

Scorched Earth, The Germans on the Somme 1914–1918: Renz, Irina, Krumeich, Gerd and Hirschfeld, Gerhard, Pen and Sword, 2009

Sir Douglas Haig's Despatches (December 1915–April 1919): Boraston, Lieutenant Colonel J.H., J.M. Dent & Sons Ltd, 1919

Tanks on The Somme from Morval to Beaumont Hamel: Pidgeon, Trevor, Pen and Sword, 2010

The 23rd Division 1914–1919: Sandilands, Lieutenant Colonel H.R., William Blackwood and Sons, 1925. Reprinted by The Naval & Military Press.

The Fifteenth (Scottish) Division 1914–1919: Stewart, Lieutenant Colonel J and Buchan, J, William Blackwood and Sons, 1926. Reprinted by The Naval & Military Press.

The German Army on the Somme 1914–1916: Sheldon, Jack, Pen and Sword, 2007

The History of the 47th (London) Division 1914–1919: Maud, Alan H, The Amalgamated Press (1922) Ltd. Reprinted by The Naval & Military Press.

The History of the 50th Division: Wyrall, Everard, Percy Lund Humphries & Co. Ltd, 1939

The History of the 9th (Scottish) Division: Ewing, John, John Murray, 1921

The Somme 1916: Gladden, Norman, William Kimber and Co. Limited, 1974

The Somme and the Butte de Warlencourt Memorial Dedication Issue – 1990: The Western Front Association, The Western Front Association, 1990

The Somme Battlefields, A Guide to the Cemeteries and Memorials of the Battlefields of the Somme 1914–1918: Scott, Michael, The Naval & Military Press

The Somme Battlefields: Middlebrook, Martin & Mary, Viking, 1991

The Somme – The Day by Day Account: McCarthy, Chris, Brockhampton Press, 1998

The Story of the 6th Battalion the Durham Light Infantry: Ainsworth, Capt. R. B., The St. Catherine Press, 1919. Project Gutenberg eBook www.gutenberg.net, 2005

The Story of the South African Brigade (abridged version of History of the South African Forces in France): Buchan, J, T Maskew Miller, 1921

Through French Eyes: The British Expeditionary Force and the Records of the French Postal Censor 1916–1918: Gibson, Craig, History Workshop Journal, No. 55 (Spring, 2003), pp. 177–188, OUP, 2003

Twelve Days: The Somme November 1916: Rogerson, Sidney, Gliddon Books, 1988

Walking the Somme: Second Edition: Reed, Paul, Pen and Sword, 2018

When the Barrage Lifts: Gliddon, Gerald, Leo Cooper, 1990

French Language Sources

Bapaume et son Canton: Roussel, Olivier, Alan Sutton, 2005

L'Abbaye d'Eaucourt: Pignon, J, Richard Boidon, 1965

Le Bilan de la Guerre 1918–1918, Journal des Mutilés et Combattants, Musée Somme 1916

Précis historique de la ville de Bapaume: Langlebert, Gabriel, Le Livre d'histoire-Lorisse Paris, 2010

German Language Sources

Zwischen Arras und Péronne: Corps Publishing House Bapaume, R. Piper & Co. Verlag, 1917

Internet

The Long, Long Trail: www.longlongtrail.co.uk

Selective Index

200